AN EMMY AWARD–WINNING ANCHOR'S
INCREDIBLE JOURNEY OF FAITH OVER FEAR

A DIRT ROAD
TO SOMEWHERE

ROMONA ROBINSON

Halo
PUBLISHING
INTERNATIONAL

Part of the proceeds will be donated to organizations
I'm passionate about that serve the needs of children of all ages.

Contact Romona Robinson:
Website: romonarobinson.com
Telephone: 800-296-8232

ISBN: 978-1-61244-559-5
Library of Congress Control Number: 2017907332

Printed in the United States of America

Halo Publishing International
1100 NW Loop 410
Suite 700 - 176
San Antonio, Texas 78213
Toll Free 1-877-705-9647
www.halopublishing.com
E-mail: contact@halopublishing.com

God places gifts in your path;
it is up to you to recognize them.

Romona Robinson

From the Author

At the heart of this book is the message that not every closed door we encounter is a bad thing. God knows that as long as we're comfortable, we won't move. We'll stay stuck.

We don't always like it when God tests our faith. It may not feel good, and we may not understand the reasons for it, but we have to have faith God is working on our behalf, and we will come through the storm. At times, God sent turmoil, betrayal, and loss into my life in order to force me into my purpose.

My wish in writing A Dirt Road to Somewhere is that you will be moved and motivated to walk in faith and not fear. Having fear is not a sin; it is simply a strong emotion that will tear us into pieces if we sit in it. Every person who walks away from fear is strong in their own way, and they can teach us valuable lessons.

—Romona Robinson

Contents

FOREWORD   13

Chapter 1   15
IF YOU CAN'T STAND THE HEAT

Chapter 2   21
THE LESSON BEGINS

Chapter 3   27
FATHERLESS

Chapter 4   35
MOM'S REPRIEVE

Chapter 5   42
MY IDOL

Chapter 6   45
BEWARE OF PREDATORS

Chapter 7   49
FARM LIFE: THE HARSH REALITY

Chapter 8   52
MY PET, MY BREAKFAST

Chapter 9   **58**
STRESS

Chapter 10   **61**
OFF TO WORK

Chapter 11   **66**
HATERS GONNA HATE

Chapter 12   **83**
IGNORE THE NAYSAYERS

Chapter 13   **87**
COLLEGE BOUND

Chapter 14   **91**
MY OWN HENRY HIGGINS

Chapter 15   **96**
NOT EVERYONE LIKES CHANGE

Chapter 16   **99**
WELCOME TO THE WORKFORCE

Chapter 17   **103**
THE DREAM IS ALIVE

Chapter 18   **109**
OPPORTUNITY KNOCKS

Chapter 19   **115**
LIGHTS, CAMERA, AND NOT MUCH ACTION

Chapter 20   **122**
MR. PRESIDENT

Chapter 21   **124**
OCCUPATIONAL HAZARD

Chapter 22   **136**
INSIDE PRISON WALLS

Chapter 23   **142**
TIME FOR CHANGE

Chapter 24   **146**
HURRICANE CHARLIE

Chapter 25   **148**
A LESSON ON SLAVERY

Chapter 26   **150**
A GOOD MAN IS GOOD ENOUGH

Chapter 27   **155**
SHOULD I STAY OR SHOULD I GO?

Chapter 28   **160**
OUT OF A JOB

Chapter 29 **162**
HIS CHEATIN' HEART

Chapter 30 **169**
A NEW BEGINNING

Chapter 31 **172**
SHOWTIME

Chapter 32 **182**
NELSON MANDELA

Chapter 33 **185**
LITTLE RED CORVETTE

Chapter 34 **187**
UNLUCKY IN LOVE

Chapter 35 **197**
THE STIGMA MUST END

Chapter 36 **205**
HANGING MY HAT IN CLEVELAND

Chapter 37 **207**
POH BLACK FOLKS SHOULD STAY IN THEIR LANE

Chapter 38 **209**
A LETTER FROM MR. CRONKITE

Chapter 39   **211**
DIVINE INTERVENTION

Chapter 40   **218**
ROMONA'S CHILDREN

Chapter 41   **228**
PRESIDENTIAL EXCLUSIVE

Chapter 42   **232**
AN UNEXPECTED PATH

Chapter 43   **235**
FAITH OVER FEAR

EPILOGUE   **239**

ACKNOWLEDGMENTS   **243**

ABOUT ROMONA   **247**

FOREWORD

If a survivor ever needed something to keep going, A Dirt Road to Somewhere captures the universal message of perseverance and hope for anyone struggling to overcome. Romona Robinson's book is an engaging series of funny, serious, and touching life events which should have compelled her failure. But when she was told no, an inner strength and an inner faith said yes. She weaves stories of an enlightened mother rearing children in poverty, a journalism professor who never accepted excuses, and Walter Cronkite. But her devotion to the communities where she worked and anchored in broadcast journalism, especially her commitment to children, makes it a perfect book on your night table to ensure sweet dreams.

Avery Friedman,
Civil Rights Lawyer/CNN Legal Analyst

Chapter 1

IF YOU CAN'T STAND THE HEAT

The January air produced a slight chill, but the heat radiating from the sun and raucous crowd smacked me in the face as I peered out the window of our news car. It was 1987. I was a twenty-six-year-old black reporter working for WCIV-TV4 in Charleston, the home of the Confederacy. My news manager had sent me to cover a Ku Klux Klan rally nearby. I was told she hoped the assignment would make me quit.

When my photographer and I pulled up, it was as if the pages of my high school history books had come to life. The image is forever imprinted on my mind. There were dozens of white men draped in long, solid-white and multi-colored robes, their fists raised, moving in harmony, chanting about white supremacy. Sharply pointed hoods covered some of their faces. Others scowled, their faces clearly exposed, the sunlight illuminating their blue, green, and brown eyes.

On the other side of the street, a large crowd of onlookers and some angry protestors had gathered—mostly white and some black—yelling and screaming for the Klan to go home. Their faces are a blur to me now, but their impassioned pleas are not:

"The Klan isn't welcome here."

"Racism is wrong."

"Hatred? Not in our town."

I had replaced an older white male anchor on the weekends when I arrived in 1985. The staff had revered him. A colleague confided in me that some in the newsroom felt he had been pushed out to make way for me—a much younger black woman—because of quotas. With that knowledge, I worked even harder to prove I belonged there. Each morning, I arrived for work at 4:00 a.m. to anchor the six o'clock morning newscast, and many nights I also fronted the six o'clock evening live reports. My degree in journalism and three years of experience should have spoken for themselves. Most of my colleagues were friendly. Some would go out of their way to be helpful. However, I could feel the tension whenever I was in the presence of one of my news managers.

But she didn't know my story. I wouldn't quit. I couldn't. Thoughts of my inspiration since I was six years old—the legendary CBS news anchor Walter Cronkite—wouldn't let me. As a little girl from a backwoods Missouri town who had once spoken broken English, a journalist was all I had ever wanted to be. I had prayed about it. Dreamed about it. And my faith in God helped me overcome many roadblocks to get there. So, I was determined to cover the story.

My manager had told me to get a sound bite from the Grand Dragon of the Ku Klux Klan. My body was wracked with fear as I slowly got out of the car. I paused for a moment as a hundred thoughts raced through my head. *How can this be? Am I dreaming? My God, this is real!*

I had to remember to breathe. The noisy and agitated crowd was a riot waiting to happen. The police were conspicuously present with their guns holstered and billy clubs in hand. Some kept a tight leash on their K-9's, ready for any problems that might arise. Suddenly, I worried I might be trampled during a scuffle if a fight broke out, or maybe a Klansman would harm me physically because of my race.

My photographer, who was white, stared at me. I'm sure he could sense my fear. My heart was beating at least twice its normal pace. He grabbed my hand and said, "Romona, I can tell you're frightened. If you want to stay in the car, I'll go by myself, hold the microphone, and get the sound. I won't tell anyone you didn't cover the story." He was sincere.

"Really, it's okay. I'm not afraid," I said with a lump in my throat.

It was a lie. I was petrified. But I was determined to be professional, just as I had been months earlier when I interviewed the civil rights leader Reverend Jesse Jackson.

The photographer grabbed his gear, and I quietly squeezed in between members of the media—all white as I recall—standing just a few feet away from the Grand Dragon. Who was I kidding? There was nothing quiet about my arrival. At six foot one in my three-inch heels, I towered over most of the men there. I was suddenly grateful for my thirty-inch arm length, which I fully extended to keep my distance.

The Grand Dragon spewed his bigotry and verbal venom, using the words "nigger" and "Jew" seemingly every other sentence, looking right past me the entire time. I felt the weight of his words as if someone had gut-punched me. I recalled a time when my grandmother, Viola, told us horror stories about white men who rode in the night with sheets covering their heads, burning crosses and lynching blacks for sport. But this was the first time in my young life I'd ever heard someone use the N-word to my face.

I was raised during the turbulent and racially divided 1960s, so I'm not sure how I had escaped hearing it, but there it was: *nigger*. Up close and personal. I was close enough to the Grand Dragon to feel his hot breath. "The world should be rid of both niggers and Jews," he shouted.

I wondered whether he could see my body flinch with every slur. *This man is not just a racist, he is a madman!* I thought. *How could such a beautiful Carolina winter day produce such a heart of darkness?* I regretted that the state's beautiful palmetto trees were the backdrop for such evil and ugliness.

I desperately tried to hide my emotions, remembering I was a journalist. Objectivity was paramount. I was surprised he never locked eyes with me because I was staring straight into his. I looked down at this stocky man with sandy-brown hair and pale, deeply blemished skin. *Who could possess such hatred?* I wondered. *Who had raised him? What kind of parents did he have?*

Before long, several Klan members set eyes on me as I tried to make out the insignia on their robes. Some gave me menacing stares, their robes flowing in the light breeze, while they shouted relentlessly about white supremacy, fueling the roar of the protestors. The yelling and taunts of the crowd grew to a feverish pitch when the Klan began to pray, saying, "In Jesus' name."

Standing there in the midst of the tension-filled moment, watching as the police moved closer to the demonstrators, who had moved closer to the Klansmen, I started to worry that if the situation escalated and shots were fired, I could be hit in the crossfire.

Out of the blue, words from the most important person in my life—my mom—flashed through my mind. She had taught me not to hate and to treat all people with respect. I learned from her that the N-word did not apply to me. Mom also said that words could never hurt me. She was wrong. The Klan and their offensive remarks did hurt, but my burning desire to make it as a journalist helped me to stand there and take it.

* * * *

Fast-forward three decades to April 14, 2013. My morning coffee took the chill off the cool spring day. However, after a phone call I had just received, a wave of heat suddenly enveloped my head. It was the same kind of heat I had felt that day in Charleston.

I'm an eight-time Emmy Award–winning television anchor and reporter in Cleveland, Ohio, and—along with my station—the recipient of the coveted Edward R. Murrow Award for breaking one of the biggest stories in the city's history: the discovery of three women held captive for a decade by Ariel Castro. I have interviewed U.S. presidents and world dignitaries during my career. I've anchored breaking news stories, such as the September 11 terrorist attacks and the famous O. J. Simpson chase. I was at the top of my career, but all the awards and accolades I had earned couldn't help me in that moment.

My hands were shaking, and my fingers were tingling. I was having trouble breathing. I could feel my heart racing. I couldn't make sense of my thoughts, and it was difficult to form words. I screamed as tears rolled down my face. My sister had just called to tell me our mom had suffered a severe stroke and was rushed into emergency brain surgery.

Hours later, I was on a plane from Cleveland to Columbia, Missouri. As we ascended into the clouds, I tried to hide my tears from the other passengers. Fear crept into my heart, and I begged the Lord, "Please don't take my mom. I'm not ready." A deep sadness came over me as I asked myself why I hadn't spent more time with her. I lived nearly seven hundred miles away, but it was no excuse for making it home only twice a year. My mom was extremely proud of me, and she understood the demands of my job as an anchor and my work with children in the community. But it was no comfort to me then.

My entire life began to play out in my mind during the eighty-minute flight. I lay back in my seat, closed my eyes, and thought of my mom—her hard work raising eleven children as a single mother and the woman who had encouraged me and believed in my dream of becoming a journalist. Then I recalled the best lesson she had ever taught me.

Chapter 2

THE LESSON BEGINS

I was six years old.

It was a blisteringly hot, damp day in late July 1965 in Wilson City, Missouri, one of those days when even a huge oak shade tree provided no relief from the summer heat.

I had come of age, Mom told me. According to church rules, it was time to baptize my two older sisters and me. We had to be dressed by noon to make the six-mile trip to Cairo, Illinois, where we would be baptized in the Mississippi River. Mom told us to put on our ragged clothes because they wouldn't be seen under our baptismal gowns. We threw on old, faded T-shirts and torn jeans with so many holes in them it looked as if the field mice that sometimes found their way into our chest of drawers had feasted on them.

When we arrived, about three dozen church members—adults and children—were waiting for us. Most of them clutched their Bibles and were wearing their Sunday best, even though it was a Saturday morning. The men wore polyester suits and fedoras. The women looked pretty in their floral dresses, flared skirts, and polished shoes. Some of the ladies' hats were adorned with feathers, and others were bejeweled with rhinestones that glistened in the sun. I thought they were overdressed for a river baptism.

Under the bright summer sky, we lined up and prepared to walk down to the river's edge. I was drenched in sweat, shaking with fear. I didn't know how to swim. As we were led down to the swiftly moving waters of the Mississippi, I began to cry.

When we approached the river, an unbelievable stench filled my nostrils. I quickly spotted the source: a mass of rotting fish had washed up on the banks of the river. Some had their eyes and heads missing, probably torn off by predators in the murky water. I watched as the current carried the fish downstream, along with discarded beer bottles and soda cans, branches, and who knows what else. Flies, gnats, and huge, pesky mosquitoes swarmed around our heads. The air was thick with no breeze at all to carry away the disgusting smell.

We were cloaked in white gowns over our clothing, and swimming caps made from old cotton sheets were tied around our heads. We were told to remove our shoes. The small congregation from Holy Grove Baptist Church started to sing a familiar hymn:

> Wade in the water,
>
> Wade in the water, children.
>
> Wade in the water,
>
> God's gonna trouble the water.

Reverend Tyus went in first, wading ten feet or so into the river, and stretched out his massive hands like Charlton

Heston playing Moses. He motioned for the oldest girl, my sister, Brenetta—we called her Peach—to come to him. Barefoot and stumbling, her eyes wide, she entered the water and took his hands. The reverend placed one hand on her forehead and the other at the center of her back. He told her to pinch her nose with her fingers and keep her mouth closed tightly. Dipping her backward, he held her head under the filthy water as he shouted, "In the name of the Father, the Son, and the Holy Ghost!" It seemed like minutes passed, although it lasted only a few seconds.

When she re-emerged, Peach looked as if she had seen a ghost underwater. She was extremely animated, flapping her hands, gasping and coughing, and spitting up the soiled water. *I guess she didn't keep her mouth closed*, I thought to myself. She looked as if she could hardly breathe. Her cap had come off and floated downstream. A few people in the congregation laughed; Peach sure did look a mess.

Peach's reaction frightened me. I started to cry a little, but I was relieved when it was my sister Evonne's turn. Evonne was only seven years old, but she had the bravery of a much older girl. Evonne wasn't afraid of anybody or anything—not spiders, not snakes, not stray dogs. Nothing. But on this afternoon, she sure seemed nervous. Nevertheless, she threw her head up, stuck out her bony chest, clutched her fists, and even smiled when Reverend Tyus lifted her head back out of the water. Mom looked at her, smiling proudly.

Then all eyes turned to me.

My tears had dried, but now I was shivering, knowing what lurked beneath the cloudy, stinky water as the reverend summoned me forward. I knew snakes, eels, frogs, and those evil-looking catfish Mom and I sometimes caught when food was scarce were down there. Reverend Tyus cut an intimidating figure; he was a large man with a deep, powerful, burly voice. All of us kids obeyed the reverend. That's how we were raised. Mom told us he was a man of God and that we should listen to him and do what he said.

As the reverend beckoned me into the water, my legs trembled. I could feel the fish darting beneath the waist-high water, banging into my legs and ankles. My bare feet stepped on rocks and sticks, bottles and mud, and the slimy, greenish goop grown-ups called seaweed. I remember how warm the water felt and the sweat dripping down my face. The closer I got to Reverend Tyus, the higher the water rose, reaching above my waist. My knees started to buckle. I stretched out my hands to steady myself.

I had seen this ritual take place time and time again. Mom had told us, "All God's children have to be baptized. Once you give your life to the Lord, He will watch over you and give you the strength and faith you need to survive anything."

The reverend's giant hands swallowed my tiny fingers as he took hold of me.

"Do you accept Jesus Christ as your Lord and Savior?" he asked.

Still shaking, my eyes wide, I blurted out, "Yes!" if only to end the torment of the awful river baptism.

Mom looked on, pleased, and the choir continued to sing. I couldn't wait to get out of the water. The murky river had soiled my clothes, and I reeked of its odor.

I didn't feel any different being saved, but it would become a defining moment for me.

* * * *

After the baptism, we drove home to Wilson City, the place where I grew up, a town so small it wasn't on the map and didn't even have a zip code. It was a place 212 people called home. Our family accounted for twelve of them. It consisted of a single dirt road lined by no more than sixty homes that were sandwiched between the highway and hundreds of acres of corn and soybean fields. Mom used to say it was the road to nowhere, but she was determined to get us somewhere. There was one way in and only one way out.

Our town was about 250 miles southeast of St. Louis. To get there, you had to travel down Interstate 55 to the southeastern tip of Missouri, the "boot hill" region. Once you reached Route 60, the pungent scent of manure and acres of crops signaled you were close. It was important to pay strict attention to the road signs or else you might drive right past it.

A few of the wood-planked homes were new, while others were shacks that should have been condemned. You could always find clothes hanging out to dry in the breeze and freshly laid hen eggs for sale on the side of the road. It was not uncommon to see a hog running loose or a couple of feisty roosters flapping about, chasing a stray dog that had ventured into their coop. Old Cadillacs sat on front lawns, perched on cinder blocks as trophies from yesteryear, reminders of a prized possession that once was. You might see a few unemployed men taking a swig of moonshine, trying to drown the harsh realities of life in our depressed little world. You might even see an old woman parked in her rocking chair on her front porch, chewing tobacco and spitting into the can in her hand—that is, if you could see her through the chest-high weeds. It was a place where half-dressed kids splashed in muddy ditches, thankful the rains had brought them make-believe swimming pools.

Just about everybody in my hometown struggled to make ends meet. We cleaned houses, mowed lawns, or worked whatever odd jobs we could find. Some became farmers to supplement their income, raising animals in their backyards and selling fruit and vegetables at makeshift stands. The median income was somewhere south of $10,000. But for me, it was home, and it would be years before I was old enough to realize that the way we lived was somehow less than the way other people did.

* * * *

Nowadays, as a successful Cleveland anchor, you might find me with perfectly coiffed hair and makeup in one of my favorite BCBG dresses and Chanel jewelry. You might figure growing up in such poverty must have been embarrassing or shameful, but that's not true. I've never forgotten the struggle and hard work of the people I grew up with. I share with them the tenacity that fuels me to this day.

Chapter 3
FATHERLESS

I have a sweet recollection of my mom from when I was a toddler: the soft touch of her hands and her warm embrace as she spoon-fed me a cold remedy of whiskey, tea, and honey she heated in a cast-iron pot on our stove. It seemed to have immediate medicinal powers, curing my cold within twenty-four hours. Or maybe I just said so because I knew on her salary that seeing a doctor was out of the question.

Being sick was the only time we got to have a sleepover in Mom's bed, and snuggling with her was like heaven, a place she described as beautiful, where there was no sickness or pain, a place we'd all want to go to be with God someday.

I have no such memories of my dad. Mom asked that I not write about her relationship with my father. He has long since passed away, and in any case, this book is about God, Mom, and me. Mom always said she birthed us into the world, and it was her job to take care of us, although I always felt it was an excuse to avoid facing the heartache and pain life had dealt her.

Born in 1934, my mother, Henrietta Robinson, was a tall, beautiful, brown-skinned woman with coarse, black hair and eyes that seemed to see straight through you to your soul. Her curves and long, gorgeous legs gave men pause and made women take notice. She married once, but it didn't last.

The father she had loved and worshipped died when she was twelve years old. From that day on, she felt lonely and abandoned. Her mother—my grandmother—Viola, drank a lot. I mean, a lot. Our visits to Grandma didn't always include ice cream or cookies. She could be nice and loving, but she would also yell at us if we refused to take a swig of whiskey. She sold my grandfather's farm and opened a juke joint, a club where patrons could drink, gamble, and dance morning, noon, and night. Mom and her thirteen siblings were mostly left home alone to fend for themselves.

Despite raising so many children on her own—ten girls and one boy to be exact—Mom had a peace about her. Mostly. It wasn't a façade; her attractive exterior simply did not reveal the backbreaking, finger-numbing factory work she did for thirty dollars a day or waitressing on her feet all day for five- and ten-cent tips. Even as a child, I recognized that Mom struggled endlessly.

Before I was born, she had worked at a nursing home, cleaned houses, and worked in the soybean, corn, and cotton fields. She used to tell me stories about how she had worked alongside her siblings, filling big sacks of cotton. Arduous work. The heavier the sack, the more money you made—about five to ten dollars a day.

In 1971, she was considered one of the lucky blacks in our town when she landed a job as a topstitch seamstress in nearby Charleston, Missouri—population 6,000—at the largest manufacturer in town, Brown Shoe Company, which was not known for its diversity in the workplace.

The factory turned out hundreds of shoes each day. As the cutters sent the shoe leather down the assembly line in buckets, Mom would retrieve them and perform the stitching on her huge industrial sewing machine. She always said leather was the toughest material to maneuver, and the stitch required perfect measurements. For precision, Mom had to bend over in order to pull and stretch the leather to keep it straight, being careful not to pierce her finger with the giant needle (this repetitive motion would later cause Mom excruciating pain in her hands and back). When she was done, the stitched fabric was placed back on the line and sent down to the fancy stitchers until a complete shoe was made. She did this for eight to ten hours a day. It was hard work made harder by the stress of being a single mom needing to care for her children. We surely could have survived on welfare, but Mom was determined to care for us herself.

Her wages at the shoe factory were not enough. Mom went to the grocery store for essentials mostly, such as bread, milk, and butter. She did qualify for some assistance. I would salivate standing in line with Mom in Charleston at the community center, waiting for our turn to be handed commodity cheese, beans, and Spam. Those were my favorites. Thick, yellow cheese grilled between two slices of buttered bread was better than any gift Mom could have bought for me. Just the smell of canned Spam being fried would send me running to the kitchen, begging for a slice on bread smeared with mayonnaise.

In our mostly barren backyard—part grass, part rocks, and part dirt—the smell of animal waste permeated the air, signaling what mostly helped Mom put food on our table. The smell grew stronger as you approached the old, rickety chicken coop. It leaned to one side, enclosed in a three-foot-high chicken-wire fence. I always thought that one day a good thirty-mile-an-hour wind might bring it down. But there it stubbornly stood, a six-by-twelve-foot, dry-rotted, wooden shed with two rows of four-foot planks inside that housed six chicken nests. The squawking of two dozen chickens, turkeys, and ducks was a sign that someone had entered their space. Our rabbits would hop about, feeding off any grass they could find. You could always locate our eight pigs at their trough. They seemed to eat all the time.

With most of our money going toward bills, Mom scoured the Goodwill and managed to find a few quality items, paying a couple of dollars apiece for articles of clothing. I remember walking the aisles of the store with her, my face planted on her hip as she nudged me not to be shy and try on the clothing other people had donated. The rest of my clothes were hand-me-downs. Mom never gave any gifts to us kids. We clamored for toys we saw on television or saw other kids playing with, but Mom always said she wouldn't buy for one of us if she couldn't buy for us all. She never did buy me a toy or a birthday or Christmas gift. Ever. I was never afforded a birthday party, and I never complained. Living in extreme poverty made me appreciate the small things, like the rare times we got to have Cheerios instead of the cheaper corn flakes, which got soggy quickly if you didn't eat them fast. Or when someone for whom my mom cleaned house gave her an old rag doll with a missing arm she was about to throw away. I beamed with joy when Mom said the doll was mine.

For years, Evonne and Peach and I got creative, making our own toys from discarded objects we found around the house. We'd make homemade Ken and Barbie paper dolls. We waited for Mom to throw out her old Sears & Roebuck catalog. Then we would carefully cut out the vanilla-colored models that resembled Ken and Barbie and lay them flat on pieces of cardboard, tracing them with a pencil. Then we'd use Elmer's glue to paste the two together. If we couldn't find any Elmer's, we used homemade honey and let them dry in the sun.

Ken and Barbie even had their own mode of transportation. We built them a car out of a discarded shoebox so they could cruise around the house. We punched a hole in the middle of one end, threaded a string through it, and tied a knot to secure it. Then we cut out four cardboard tires about three inches in diameter and hitched them to the sides of the box with glue. The wheels didn't roll, but that was okay. We just dragged Ken and Barbie in and out of our bedrooms, pretending there were candy stores and shops along the way.

We made a great creative team, the three of us, yet we were so different.

Evonne was a year older than me. She was the rebel in the family, the ringleader. Trouble just seemed to find her.

She was always ready, willing, and able to fight someone who had made her mad, and she was fiercely protective of me. You could say she and I were joined at the hip; you didn't see one without the other. We wore our hair the same way: three braided ponytails, one in the front and two in the back. Through trial and error and wasting a lot of Mom's good flour and sugar, Evonne learned to bake the best peanut butter and sugar cookies you ever tasted.

Peach, two years older than me, had a slender, athletic build and loved sports and music. She played the piano at school and unfortunately brought a flute home to practice one day. She could clear out a room with the high-pitched, ear-numbing sound that blared throughout our tiny home. Then she turned to the trumpet. She would blow so hard I swear a stampede of elephants came trampling through. I wanted to be supportive, but it was just awful, and she knew it. So, she decided to run track instead. We were all grateful.

I was known as the shy, nice one. Number six—right in the middle. Unlike my slender sisters, I was pudgy. I was the odd-looking, inquisitive one who cried easily and never found a book I didn't want to read. I always had my face planted in the pages of a book or a magazine I had dug out of the neighbor's trash, even if the pages were missing or stained with dried, week-old food. *Charlotte's Web*, *The Three Little Pigs*, or *Reader's Digest*—I would read them cover to cover. It was my passion.

Even though poverty was all we had ever known, my mom dreamed of a better life for my siblings and me. She didn't want us to struggle and have to work as hard as she did. Being poor didn't mean she was blind to the riches she saw on television. She always preached about not wanting us to live our lives in poverty. She wanted us to have more. She didn't want us dating boys until we were seventeen or ready to graduate high school—and we were all expected to graduate high school. She wanted us to go on to college as well.

We called it "preaching" because she spoke in and out of Scripture so loudly that all of us could hear her no matter where we were in the house. Sometimes she would have tantrums, yelling, "I've got ten daughters, but hell if I'm gonna raise ten grandbabies!" She would stomp up and down our long, oakwood hallway at least once a week, preaching about the importance of education. I'm sure the repetition of her heavy footsteps is what eventually caused the floorboards to creak.

Despite her lot in life, Mom was a proud, strong woman. To this day, her work ethic has rivaled that of anyone I've ever met. She had inherited her daddy's might and grit, working hard and having faith in God that things would get better. She said my grandfather had saved up enough money from working in the fields in the 1940s to buy a parcel of land, land he worked with just one mule and a plow. Mom always smiled proudly when she talked about her dad. He was her inspiration.

In 1965, when she was thirty-one years old, Mom bought a piece of the American dream. She paid $170 for an empty lot and made a $250 down payment on a small, white, newly built, $7,500 house, courtesy of a low-income loan from the Federal Housing Authority. It sat at the end of the dirt road.

All eight of us at the time crammed into the nearly 1,200 square-foot home with four bedrooms and one bathroom.

Home ownership was a dream come true for Mom. It gave her a tremendous sense of pride and accomplishment. She had dreamed of it since having her first child at sixteen. She had prayed for it. She had ached for it. She never thought it was possible, even though she had saved for years, putting away two to five dollars a month whenever she could. She told us it was only by the grace of God and the kindness of a neighbor who had believed in her and showed her how to pursue her dream.

Mom taught me that sometimes God places gifts in your path; however, it's up to you to recognize them.

Chapter 4
MOM'S REPRIEVE

I don't ever remember any playtime for Mom. Going out to nightclubs or partying with friends was never an option. She would come home from work exhausted, her back aching from bending over her sewing machine all day. Her fingers were tired to the bone from wrestling with cowhide fabrics. But she did have two things she coveted: her Bible and Walter Cronkite. And she didn't like to be disturbed from either one.

Every night, she kicked off her shoes and snuggled into her comfortable brown chair to watch *CBS Evening News* with Walter Cronkite, the veteran television journalist. He was known as "the most trusted man in America." If Mister Cronkite reported it, it must be true, Mom used to say. When he spoke, Mom listened intently, sometimes leaning forward in her chair, insisting everyone hush when the news came on. She revered him.

Mom and I had developed a special bond watching the evening news together. She said our TV time was a ritual we had practiced since I was four years old. I would climb into her lap and point at the pictures on the screen. I don't remember doing that, but I do recall that when I was in kindergarten, she used to yell, "Romona! Walter Cronkite is on!"

With my other siblings playing outside most days, I would go running inside to our small, wood-paneled living room with a big smile plastered on my face and plant my tiny frame right beside Mom in her favorite chair. It was covered with an old throw she'd put over our legs if there was a chill in the room. She became animated when she explained to me what was going on in the world—all of the turmoil of the late 1960s.

"We're in the middle of the civil rights movement, and that man they're showin' there on television is civil rights leader Dr. Martin Luther King," I remember her saying. "He's fightin' for betta opportunities and jobs for black folks, and he believes in doing it without violence. You can tell Dr. King has great faith. He's not fearful of trying to bring about change."

I also recall with great clarity watching and being moved by a recording of Dr. King's famous 1963 "I Have a Dream" speech. I especially loved the part when he said he hoped "one day, right here in Alabama, little black boys and black girls will be able to join hands with little white boys and white girls as sisters and brothers."

At just eight years old, those words resonated through my tiny body, filling me up with so much hope that maybe someone at the school I was bussed to every day would play with me. By 1967, most states had integrated their public school systems. In Charleston, Mom said they had started on a trial basis, bussing the top ten percent of black students to nearby all-white elementaries.

I was one of about a dozen of these students. My first day of school was intense. The white kids threw wadded-up paper at us in class and never spoke to us. They only stared. The teachers kept all of us black children in the front of class to protect us. The black boys had it worse. They were shoved and called names: *sambo, blackie, dirty.*

The worst thing that ever happened to me took place on the playground: experiencing the sound of laughter as other kids screamed to go higher on the swings and climbed the monkey bars, fun I would not experience. For weeks during recess, I stood outside the door next to my teacher. I can't picture her face now, but I can recall the image of me holding onto her floral skirt and the smell of her flower-scented perfume. I was the only black girl at recess. The two black boys played together.

Then, suddenly, there she was: strawberry-blonde hair, pale skin, gapped teeth, and a big smile. Emily, I believe her name was. Her last name escapes me. "Romona, you wanna come play?" she asked with joy in her eyes. I actually froze for a moment. I thought I would burst I was so happy.

"Come on," she said, grabbing my hand, literally pulling me over to the seesaw. The color of my skin didn't seem to bother Emily as we bounced up and down, few words spoken, just two little girls holding on with one hand and reaching for the heavens with the other. I've thought about Emily over the years. I wish I could find her and tell her the impact she had on my life that day.

The alarming images I saw on television also had an impact on me. There were raging fires, people fighting, and policemen wielding billy clubs while restraining their dogs. Mom said it was all because some whites wanted to deny us the right to jobs, good housing, and the right to vote.

One evening, I was fixated by pictures of the Detroit riot of 1967, one of the largest and deadliest riots in our nation's history. Mom didn't bother to shield me from the horrific tales of beatings, robberies, and killings. There were images of raging fires that burned down businesses and cars and police in riot gear clashing with protestors. Days later, I watched hundreds of National Guardsmen in riot gear on TV walking through the streets with guns drawn. It was frightening, but I was engrossed.

Television news was like an addiction; I had to have it every day. Mom was amazed but intrigued by my fascination, and she was eager to provide a daily history lesson. She would teach me what had happened in the past and why Dr. King was so determined to create change for blacks. Mom really liked this man. Just the mention of Dr. King's name would send her scurrying to the television, and she hung on his every word. It was as if Dr. King was a member of our family. I remember asking Mom whether we could meet Dr. King and his family and Mr. Cronkite since she liked them so much.

"No, baby. Poh black folk like us down here on this dirt road in the sticks can't meet people like that," she said.

I don't ever remember lighthearted baby talk. She talked to me like I was an adult, engaging me in serious conversations about life and the political climate of our country. I had questions about the turbulent world I was living in.

"They're gonna kill him," she said one day, glued to the TV.

"Who, Momma?" I asked, grabbing her arm, feeling like I would burst if she didn't answer quickly.

"Dr. King. They're gonna kill that man," she said again.

I had so many questions: *Do the people who hate Dr. King hate us, Momma? Are they gonna kill us, too? Do all white people hate us? What does "as-sass-i-na-tion" mean, Momma?*

Mom almost always had the answer, but when she didn't, she'd admit it.

I recall vividly the evening Dr. King was shot: April 4, 1968. She yelled for all of us to come to the living room. "Come in here, all of y'all. Dr. King has been shot in Memphis," she shouted.

I remember the look of horror and utter shock on Mom's face as she watched the news, one hand over her chest and tears welling up in her eyes. I think it was the first time I had ever seen her cry. She had always appeared so strong, never showing fear, but not on this day.

"They done shot him and we gotta pray that he lives," she said. "He knew he was gonna die," Momma kept repeating out loud.

"How did he know, Momma?" my sisters and I asked.

"He said it on TV in Memphis last night speakin' to some garbage workers who were on strike. Oh, Lawd!" she kept saying as her body swayed back and forth in her favorite chair. "He told them workers he was not concerned about his own life and being killed. He just wanted to keep fightin' fo' our rights. I knew he sounded like he knew he was gonna die," she wailed. "Lawd, Lawd, Lawd help him. Don't let him die," Momma prayed.

She instructed us to huddle together and bow our heads in prayer. There were six or seven of us in the house then, and with hands linked, surrounding Mom, we just prayed for several minutes.

But an hour later, they announced on *CBS Evening News* that the doctors couldn't save Dr. King. He was dead. Mom became verbally hysterical, shouting a mixture of curse words and incomplete Scripture in the same breath. "All he wanted was to give us a fair chance. That man did not deserve to die. They've gotta find the motherf***s who did this. No weapon formed against us. There are gonna be riots…"

She had risen from her chair and was walking around the living room in a teary-eyed daze. The room erupted in cries from all of my sisters, my brother, and me. Even my baby siblings, who I knew were too young to know what was happening, were wailing. No one was in control that evening. We tried hugging Mom, but she was inconsolable. I just remember her locking the doors and telling us to go to bed early because Dr. King's assassination might bring trouble that evening.

I still get chills thinking about what Dr. King said the night before he was killed:

> Like anybody, I would like to live a long life. Longevity has its place. But I'm not concerned about that now…I've seen the promised land. I may not get there with you. But I want you to know

tonight, that we, as a people, will get to
the promised land!

—Dr. Martin Luther King Jr.

April 3, 1968

It was at such times, like so many others, that Mom
kept her Bible close. I wanted to know more about this big,
burgundy, torn-and-worn, duct-tape bandaged book with
scratched notes and underlined Scriptures inside. *What is so
special about it? Why does it seem to comfort Momma so much?*

I noticed that every time she closed it, she would say,
"God will make a way out of no way." Of course, I had no
idea what that meant.

One evening, I eased into Mom's bedroom and climbed
up beside her as she lay propped up on a pillow. I could
tell she was comfortable and in a good mood, so I asked
if I could read her Bible. She was immediately impressed
that I was interested.

"You can't read this yet, Romona," she said, smiling.

"Uh-huh, yes I can," I remember saying.

"Okay, come on up here and read something to me."

The Bible was hard to understand. Many of the words
looked weird to me, and I couldn't comprehend what they
meant. But as the weeks and months went by, I learned to
sound out "Je-rus-a-lem," "Deu-te-ron-o-my," and "Co-
rin-thi-ans."

Mom would flash a big smile when I read to her. It
pleased her, and I loved it.

Chapter 5
MY IDOL

There were three influential men in our house as I saw it: God, Dr. Martin Luther King Jr., and Walter Cronkite.

This Mr. Cronkite of Mom's piqued my curiosity. I was drawn to his style. He seemed honest and was always calm, even when he read breaking news. He had a soothing voice. He also had huge eyes. But I liked how his bushy eyebrows lifted up as he delivered important news. I especially looked forward to the end of the news hour. I would mimic him, trying to sync my lips to his voice as he delivered his departing catchphrase: "That's the way it is, Tuesday, November twenty-sixth."

"I want to be just like him!" I had declared a few years earlier at six years old after watching *CBS Evening News* one night. "I'm gonna read the news one day, Momma," I shouted again with a huge smile, my arms waving in the air.

"You are my smart baby," she said. I remember her smiling and looking down at me, thankful that at least one of her children was already planning her future.

"I want to go to college, too. UCLA!" I belted out.

"Okay, baby, you can go to college," she said, still smiling.

I wasn't even sure what college was, but Mom was constantly talking about all of us attending a four-year university. I had seen a television commercial that showed some kids saying, "Come to UCLA!" They looked friendly, as if they were enjoying college. That image stuck with me, and I had decided that was where I wanted to go.

"You know, you have to go to school and get really good grades to go to college," Mom said as she rose from her chair.

"I know, Mom," I said, looking back at her with determination in my eyes. I was quite the dreamer. I always managed to find a quiet place for just my thoughts and me. I dreamed of becoming a journalist. I dreamed of meeting and interviewing important people, like presidents and the actors I watched on TV. I dreamed of wearing fancy clothes I paid for myself, not charity ones, even though I was grateful for them. And even as a child, with all I witnessed on television, I dreamed of peace between blacks and whites in our country.

* * * *

My love of reading and my determination at school seemed to bring Mom comfort in a life that was anything but comfortable. "My Romona, she's gettin' all A's up there at school, and she said she's goin' to college and she can pronounce big words real good, even in the Bible," Mom boasted to the neighbors, beaming with pride.

It drove my siblings crazy when I'd practice big words aloud in front of the television. As soon as the credits started rolling after our favorite shows, I would prop up on the sofa, frantically trying to get out every name before it scrolled off screen. "Bonanza! Starring Lorne Green! Little Joe Cartwright, played by Michael Landon!" I raised my voice theatrically, sounding out the names and pronouncing each syllable perfectly while my sisters pleaded for me to be quiet. I don't know why it brought me so much joy.

Maybe I was just being a show-off because I could. Or maybe Mom's reprieves had become my own. Along with our shared love of Walter Cronkite, I prayed a lot when I was alone, asking God to help Mom take care of us. She was so tired after work and never had enough energy to play with us. And she was always worrying about something— not enough food, too many bills, or a sick child. Late at night, when she thought we were asleep, all Mom had to keep her company was her faith in God. I could hear her praying out loud, asking for God's help. She would shout, "Lawd, Lawd, Lawd, help me! I know you'll make a way out of no way."

I had learned from Reverend Tyus that God loves all of His children, and He would take care of me. "Just pray and have faith and call on Him for help, no matter what the situation or problem," he'd say. I learned to embrace his preaching, as my mom did before me.

Chapter 6
BEWARE OF PREDATORS

As much as I loved school, attending classes in modular trailers caused me a lot of angst. I wasn't sure why. I liked my teacher, who was always excited to see the dozen or so boys and girls marching out to class. Enrollment had swelled at my elementary, so in fourth grade, they used the single-story, prefab structures as separate classrooms behind the school. Only a handful of kids could squeeze into the claustrophobic trailers perched precariously on concrete blocks. There was little insulation, and when the wind blew, the structures were shaky, noisy, and drafty. Regular wooden desks were abandoned in favor of plastic and metal tables that lined the trailer walls.

Our teacher, a tall, slim man with short, cropped hair and a mustache, was about thirty years old. He would walk around and slide into a chair next to each student, working with us individually. When he sat next to me, there wasn't much space between us. He sat very close, looking like the Jolly Green Giant in a chair clearly fit for a child. I could feel the warmth of his huge body as he pressed tightly against me. Sometimes his thigh would slip over the top of mine, and he would wiggle it back and forth in between my tiny legs. At times, I would close my legs tightly and try to scoot away to avoid the awkward intimacy. But then he would intensely and forcefully pry open my much smaller legs with his massive thighs.

At nine years old, I didn't understand why this was happening, and I was afraid to ask him to move his leg. One day, I was surprised to be called to the principal's office, where my mom and another teacher were waiting for me. *Someone is in big trouble,* I thought, *but it can't be me. I haven't done nothin' wrong!* Even so, they had serious looks on their faces.

"Sit down, Romona," the principal said. "We want to talk to you about something very important." Scared, I said nothing, looking at my mom, who was staring back at me. It was the middle of the day, long before quitting time for Momma, so I knew if she had been called off work for something I had done, my punishment would be harsher than anything my principal could do to me.

"Has your teacher ever touched you…inappropriately? In the trailer?" the principal asked calmly but sternly.

"I'm not sure what 'in-ap-pro-pri-ate-ly' means," I replied slowly, not knowing how to answer.

"Let me ask you another way. Has he ever done anything to make you nervous or uncomfortable while you were in the trailer?"

The three of them leaned in, waiting for my response. That's when I told them about the wiggling. I described in detail how his leg would flop over mine and the constant wiggling motion I didn't like. It felt strange and made me nervous.

The female teacher who was there said gently, "Of course, his leg could accidentally fall on top of yours. He's much taller. Right, Romona? Is that what happened?" she asked.

The principal, a very tall man, said, "I'm going to sit close to you, if it's okay with your mom, and allow my leg to rub next to yours, and you tell me if that's what happened." Mom nodded yes, it was okay. I was tight-lipped during the whole exercise as my principal's leg bumped my thigh and knee a few times.

"You see, my leg touched yours by accident," he confidently explained.

"But his thigh completely covered mine, resting in between my legs, prying them open, and he shook back and forth," I responded. Apparently, I was quite convincing.

Later, I learned the reason for all the bizarre questions. Our teacher had been accused of fondling another elementary school student in the trailer, touching her in private places. He had never done those things to me.

As I left the office, my principal asked that I not discuss the meeting with my peers. However, Mom later told me that every student who had lessons in my teacher's trailer or had any contact with him was questioned.

Shortly afterward, the teacher disappeared from school. No one ever knew what happened to him. Mom was extremely upset that I hadn't told her what happened, but as a child, I had no idea he was doing anything wrong. We never had sex education or the awareness children have today about appropriate and inappropriate touching.

This should serve as a cautionary tale. Looking back, I realize my teacher must have been grooming me by being overly kind, getting close, and gaining my trust, as I now know child predators do. Even though I could not see the danger then, God did, and He was watching over me, just as my mom said He always would.

Chapter 7

FARM LIFE: THE HARSH REALITY

The episode at school soon became a distant memory. After all, I had many responsibilities at home. My after-school chores were grueling. Some kids might mow the lawn or do the dishes, but in my house, my siblings and I had to care for our animals, collect eggs from the chicken coop, and clean the pigpen and henhouse. We survived on the meat and eggs from the animals we raised, and we also earned money from selling extra chicken eggs. Our dinner almost always consisted of some form of chicken—fried chicken, baked chicken, chicken dumplings, chicken salad, chicken and gravy, chicken stew. Any way you could prepare it, we did.

Actually killing a hen for our dinner, though, was the worst. There are two ways to kill a hen: you can ring its neck until its head pops off, or you can stretch the hen's neck over a block of wood and chop its head off with an ax. Although the latter method is faster and cleaner, it seemed especially barbaric to me. I preferred to spin the bird around until its head separated from its body.

I was more afraid of grabbing the hens in the first place. They would peck at us with their sharp beaks five or six times before we could catch one. Some days, if I could come up with five cents, my brother, Danny, would kill the bird for me. We always had to pay him, though; he wouldn't do anything for free.

I remember the first time I had to catch and kill a hen for dinner. I cried the whole time. My older sisters showed me how to hold its neck tightly in my hand without letting it go and spin my arm around until the neck and head severed. Some days I'd drop it because the neck would heat up in my hand, and the more I spun it around, the more it felt wet and slimy! But my mom had taught us it was cruel not to finish the job quickly. We didn't want the animals to suffer.

I also dreaded collecting fresh eggs every day. When it was my turn, there was always drama. "A snake! Momma, a snake!" I'd scream as I came running out of the henhouse. I nicknamed it the "haunted house" because it was dark inside with intricately cast spider webs that seemed to span three or four feet in diameter. There were bats and huge rodents that from time to time would send Mom running out with her hands in the air, screaming.

But on that day, Mom was standing at the back door, pointing her finger as I ran toward her.

"If you don't get yo' little butt back in there and bring those hen eggs in here, Romona!" she shouted angrily.

"But Momma, there's a big ol' looonnnggg snake curled around the eggs, and it hissed at me!" I said, starting to cry.

"Romona, you do this every time. You know it's just a garden snake. Get a stick and push it aside. I'm not playin' with you, Romona. Go get my hen eggs," she warned, hands on her hips, slamming the back door shut.

I knew I needed to be strong. Plus, Reverend Tyus had taught us to pray whenever we were afraid. As I crept back to the chicken coop, I bowed my head and prayed the snake wouldn't strike me.

My sisters' faces were plastered against the screen of the back window. I could hear Peach whisper, "Romona, she won't let us come help you this time."

"Mom said you gotta learn to do it yourself," Evonne chimed in. They knew what I knew: either get the hen eggs or go get a switch (translation: tree limb) from our big maple tree and get a whipping. Of course, I would rather face a hundred garden snakes than Mom armed with a switch.

My heart was pounding as I reached the door to the henhouse. The roosters and hens were frenzied. The multicolored snake, with hues of brown, cream, and black, might have been beautiful if it weren't for those evil eyes. Its three-foot-long body—or maybe it was four feet—was coiled around the eggs. I was in luck. It had already started swallowing an egg, its jaw stretched wide, so it couldn't strike me. Still, even with a lump in its throat from the egg, it looked menacing, like the devil. Standing on my tiptoes, I reached over into the hen's nest, pushed the snake aside with a stick, and snatched the fresh eggs. The snake slithered and wagged its tail end, its eyes locked on mine as if it were trying to hypnotize me with fear. And it did, but nothing like the fear I would feel if I cracked all of Mom's eggs.

When I emerged from the henhouse, Evonne and Peach were clapping in the window. "Romona, you did it!" they yelled. They smiled widely, and so did I.

Chapter 8

MY PET, MY BREAKFAST

The slaughter of a pig provided a special feast for my family. Unfortunately, I had a fondness for pigs, and I cringed whenever it was time to eat one of them. I had taken one as a pet in spite of Mom's stern warning not to. She dealt in reality. Farm animals were essential to our survival. But when our sow gave birth to a beautiful, light-caramel-colored baby with a fat, curly tail, I had to have her. I named her Missy. Every time I pulled her tail to try and straighten it, it would pop right back into a curl. Her cute nose, her big, floppy ears, and her pretty, dark eyes made her irresistible. I loved how she oinked at me every day when I fed her siblings and her. She always ate from my hand.

Even though Mom forbade it, I brought Missy into the house and hid her under my bed in the afternoons after I finished my homework and before Mr. Cronkite came on. I quickly learned how smart pigs were. I taught Missy to obey commands, like "hide" when we heard Mom coming. When I put my finger to my lips and said "quiet," she would dart underneath my bed. I took some of Mom's old baby bottles and snuck milk from the fridge to feed her. I would put her in my bed and say "lie down," and she would.

One day, when Missy was hiding safely in my room—or so I thought—I heard a sudden scream as Mom called my name down the hallway.

"Romona, do you have that pig in this house?" she asked, her heavy footsteps stomping to my room.

I was always afraid to lie to Mom, so I drew silent. I put my finger to my mouth to signal Missy to be quiet and still because there was no time to say "hide." As Mom reached my doorway, I threw my bedspread over Missy.

"Where is she, Romona? Where's that damn pig?" Mom said, huffing and puffing. "I know she's in here. The evidence is all down my hallway."

Apparently, Missy had left a wet trail leading straight into my room.

"Give me that pig, Romona," she said, and I was sure I was just a few seconds away from a bad spanking.

My bedspread moved swiftly as Missy tried to find her way out from under the covers. Mom yanked the bedspread back and screamed for Missy to get out. The pig dashed for the door and scurried down the hallway to the back door, with Mom close on her tail, flinging open the door to let her outside.

It would be my first trip to the dreaded tree. I knew the drill; I had watched my sisters and brother do it often. I walked outside to one of the huge trees, tore off a thick branch, and picked off the leaves. I walked back to the house slowly, as if I could postpone the inevitable. Crying, I handed Mom the switch she would discipline me with.

I sure had a sore butt, and my two nicknames were born: "fat pig" because I favored the pigs and because I was the chubby one, and "crybaby" because my sisters felt I cried about anything and everything.

* * * *

Missy had grown into a great big sow, and according to Mom, she had the makings of a feast. I remember the Saturday morning the neighborhood men came for her. The pig I thought of as Missy's husband—a huge, five-hundred-pound black beast—was pacing inside the pen, letting out loud, high-pitched squeals. It was as if he knew what was coming.

"Momma! Momma! Please don't let 'um kill Missy!" I begged, wrapping my arms tightly around her waist and snuggling my head between her breasts. "Not Missy!" I cried.

"Romona, didn't I tell y'all not to make them pigs pets? Didn't I?" she said gently, pushing my head back and looking down at me sternly.

"Yeah, Momma, but please, I love her!" I said, still sobbing and pleading for Missy's life.

"I'm sorry, but we've gotta eat, and I can't afford to spend no money on a lot of food," she explained.

The anguish I still feel from that moment is almost indescribable.

"Oh my God! Oh my God!" I screamed, running to my bedroom. I slammed the door and buried my head under the pillow. "I'm sorry! I didn't do it, Missy!"

The day before, I overheard Mom on the phone setting up Missy's slaughter with the neighborhood men. I had planned to sneak out to the pigpen under the cover of darkness when everyone was asleep and set her free, just as I had done for her sister a year earlier, but I didn't get the chance. They found that pig at a neighbor's, Miss Johnson's, at her back door. I'm told it scared her so badly it almost gave her a heart attack. No one ever knew how she had escaped. Mom thought it was a neighbor boy playing a prank, but it was me.

"Missy, not Missy!" I continued to cry out. My face was drenched in tears.

I could hear a flurry of activity outside my window. There were several cars outside the house, and the chickens, turkeys, and ducks were all squawking. I tried pressing a pillow against my ears to muffle the sound, but I could still hear Missy squealing. I heard the men yelling, "Grab her, corner her, get the rope around her!"

A few minutes later, there was a single shotgun blast, and I knew it was over. I also knew what would happen next because I had witnessed it many times before. They would string her up by her hind legs between two tall, wooden poles that had been erected in our backyard years ago. They would gut her down the middle with a large butcher knife, spilling out her guts and producing several weeks' worth of meat.

Picturing what was happening to my pet was almost too much to bear. I was in sheer agony. I must have cried myself to sleep because I remember waking up to find breakfast and lunch had passed me by. Despite calls from Mom to come and eat dinner, I refused to leave my room. There was no way I could ever eat Missy. I would starve first.

Standing in my doorway, Mom tried to explain once again, but I didn't want to hear it. I wanted no consolation from her.

"Go to bed then if you're gonna act like that," Mom said as she shut my door.

The next morning, I woke to the sound of Mom hollering my name and what used to be the irresistible smell of slab bacon.

"Romona, come eat breakfast," she yelled from the kitchen. "You didn't eat all day yesterday, and I'm not havin' it today. Get in here and eat somethin'!"

After washing up, I slowly made it to the table. My eyelids were fat and puffy, swollen from a marathon of crying the night before. My sisters and brother were already eating the hot, crispy bacon Mom had fried up. There were scrambled eggs with cheese and piping-hot, homemade biscuits, usually all of my favorites. I sat, staring at my plate, everyone's eyes on me. I slowly ate my biscuit and gently scooped up my eggs, careful not to let my fork touch the bacon.

"Romona, we don't waste no food in this house. Eat yo' bacon," she said, giving me the evil eye.

"I'm not hungry, Mom," I said softly, knowing it was a tale. I was half-starved.

"Don't make me have to whup yo' butt. I can't have you gettin' sick. I ain't got no money for doctor bills, so eat!" She leaned forward, looking right into my eyes.

I lifted the bacon from my plate, reluctantly placing it in my mouth as I said a silent prayer: *Please forgive me, Missy.*

There was an eruption of laughter at the table when I began to chew.

"Stop it!" Mom barked at them as I sprang from the table and ran back to my bedroom, sobbing all over again.

As much as I loved my mom and marveled at her strength, I was furious with her and with God for weeks. No amount of faith or pleading with them had saved Missy.

Chapter 9

STRESS

In my mom's defense, she had to make tough decisions in order to keep us healthy, pay bills, keep a roof over our heads, keep the lights on, and buy us essentials like winter coats. Things like scarves, hats, and gloves were luxuries, not necessities. I often wore hand-me-down shoes from my older sisters that were too small for my feet. They were so tight you could see the imprint of my toes in the worn leather. To this day, I have a dark scar on the heel of my left foot, a reminder of shoes far too small.

I remember running home from school crying, showing Mom the blisters that had formed on my ankles. Mom would double up the bandages and put them on my heels to cushion the pain. She would hug me and rock me back and forth, promising I'd get my own shoes soon. Sometimes "soon" meant six months or more.

My mom could be so warm and loving and nurturing and funny, but her words could also sting when she was angry or stressed, like the day Peach and Evonne came home with failing grades in reading and math. They were in fifth and sixth grade.

She screamed at them, pacing the hallway as I nervously peeped out from my bedroom. "I work so hard to put food on the table," she said, agitated. "The least the two of you could do is try and get good grades instead of flunkin' out at that school. Now I get a letta sayin' I have to go up to that school for a counselin' session with yo' teachers, and I can't afford to take off work," she said, waving a piece of paper in the air. Mom's voice cracked like it did when she was terribly worried about something.

"Romona, I'm tired. I need my glasses. I can't see this paper, and I've been working all day. Come read this letta and tell me what those teachers want," she yelled.

Fumbling with the paper, I brought it close to my face because I knew how important it was to read the words correctly.

"It says, Momma, that Peach and Evonne need tutoring. It also says you might have to pay for someone to teach them after school. It's what they're saying or they might not pass to the next grade," I explained sheepishly.

"I don't have no money to pay nobody to teach y'all how to read and do math," Mom explained, raising her voice forcefully. "I work all day every day tryin' to feed y'all. The least you can do is pay attention up there at that school and learn somethin'."

"Romona, take those dummies in the otha room and teach 'um how to read and do their math!" she shouted angrily.

Peach and Evonne looked sad. I didn't like it either, but I responded, as always, "Yes, Momma." We didn't dare talk back.

I felt bad for my sisters. It wasn't that they weren't smart; it was just that I had gotten a head start, quite literally. I was the first child to be enrolled in the Head Start program when I was four years old. I don't remember much about it. I recall they taught me my ABC's and numbers, and I learned to spell my name and my mom's name. It was a class for preschoolers, and it was meant to get us ready for kindergarten. I loved it because I felt grown-up, like my big sisters going to school.

Hoping to ease Mom's anxiety, I tutored Evonne and Peach every day after school. It was fun being in the fourth grade and reading books and doing math for fifth and sixth graders. I enjoyed pretending I was the teacher, although I was careful not to make my sisters feel ashamed.

Chapter 10
OFF TO WORK

At ten years old, with the fourth grade behind me, I passed the dreaded "height test." I was tall with broad shoulders, and I looked old enough to join my three sisters working ten hours a day in the soybean fields chopping beans, the annual summer job for those of us over five foot six. At that height, you could fool the prying eye of the sheriff at a distance as he drove along the highway looking for underage children working illegally. We earned about twenty dollars for a day's work. This was a way for all of us to help Mom pay the bills. Along with grants and loans, it was also how we saved money so Mom was able to provide us with a college education.

In the wee hours of the morning, before the sun rose and before our rooster's 5:30 a.m. wake-up crow, we could hear the engine of the old, beat-up pickup truck approaching the end of our dirt road to take us to work. The truck's white color was impossible to make out because of the rust and wear and tear on the body of the two-seat cab. The back was flanked by wooden boards and outfitted with benches, where we sat. The truck probably had been designed to haul feed and equipment, but instead, about twenty of us from the neighborhood would crowd in. We got bounced and tossed around with the garden hoes on the bed of the truck, filed so sharp they would cut through your shoe if they made contact with your foot during the ride out to the fields.

Our job was to separate stubborn weeds that could put a choke hold on crops and cut off proper nutrients. We dressed in old shirts and torn pants. We wore high socks to prevent the over-lapped beans from cutting and scarring our ankles and towels to protect our faces from the sun because we couldn't afford straw hats. The scorching heat bore down on our bodies as we walked acres upon acres of soybean fields with our hoes, pushing our way through lapped beans and chopping weeds in every row. The hot, blinding sun was punishing and left us with a deep, dark tan.

It was the kind of work that wreaked havoc on your entire body—excruciating back and foot pain from hours of walking, neck and shoulder aches from bending over the hoe to chop weeds, and blisters and calluses from gripping the hoe tightly.

It was tough work made tougher when we encountered a huge field snake or when one of those gigantic, black-and-yellow spiders cast a web right across our row of beans. Every day, one of us would draw laughter after screaming that we had seen a snake or the biggest spider that ever lived.

During our twenty-minute lunch break, we tore open our brown-bag lunches that Mom had packed. There were never any surprises—just cheap, saltine crackers, sardines, or Vienna sausages. We tried to find shade under a big oak tree, or if the rains had come, we'd lunch on the back of the open-air truck, many times welcoming the cool down from Mother Nature.

To pass the time, my sisters and I and the other youngsters sang the latest Motown hits or argued over which member of the Jackson 5 we loved most. Some of the old folks sang Negro spirituals.

One day, as the temperatures soared into the eighties, with the sun beating down on us and dust blowing in our sweat-drenched faces, a beautiful sight came into view. It was unlike anything we had ever seen before. It was a sleek, sporty, shiny red automobile. "Only white folk can own somethin' like that," said the boys working in the field with us. "It's called a Corvette, one of the fastest cars on Earth," they boasted as everyone stopped to look at it in awe. It was a convertible. A white man was driving, and there was a white woman in the passenger seat.

Evonne and I were spellbound as we stared at the woman in black sunglasses, her long, blonde hair blowing in the wind. The bright sunlight bounced off her face, revealing a big smile. As our supervisor yelled for us to get back to work, I said to Evonne, "One day the Lord is gonna bless me with a red Corvette, and I'm gonna put the top down and come pick you up, and we'll go for a ride around town, just like them."

The boys laughed. "Yeah right, in yo' dreams, Romona! That will be the day you drive somethin' like that!" But Evonne believed me and said she had faith that one day I would have a Corvette. Evonne and I always supported each other's dreams, no matter how far-fetched they seemed.

* * * *

At the end of our workweek, we rode into town to get paid. I dreaded the ride; it was so embarrassing. We would go into Charleston in the back of that old truck. Our classmates hung out at the general store, and they would gather at the back of the pickup to see who had been working in the fields all day for the white man only to be paid a hundred dollars a week.

What made it worse was the way we looked. After long hours in the fields, we were drenched in grime and sweat. Our old tennis shoes were filthy, soaked with mud most days. We tried hiding our faces under our work towels, but somehow the other kids always recognized us and called out to us by name.

"Evonne, Romona, Peach!" they hollered.

"I know that's y'all coverin' yo' faces," one girl said, pointing at us.

"Y'all are so poh you gotta work in the bean fields," another shouted.

"Look at all that dirt on yo' clothes, Evonne. Y'all look like slaves," a boy said, laughing hysterically.

Some days I felt so ashamed and humiliated I wanted to cry. And I did.

Other days, I laughed as my sisters fought back, trading insults with the other kids. At twelve years old, Peach had grown into a tall and intimidating girl with a bold, in-your-face personality. She could be terribly sweet, which is why my uncle had given her the nickname Peach, but you didn't want to get on her bad side.

Evonne was the chameleon of the family. She had blossomed into a beautiful girl with a perfect face and gorgeous eyes and hair. She stood about five foot seven with a slim frame. "Just like the singer, Diana Ross," people used to tell her.

Evonne made friends easily, and she liked everyone so long as you didn't mess with her sisters. She could change personalities like some people change clothes. She could be your best friend one day, but if you talked badly about her family, she became a tiger. I think Peach and Evonne enjoyed the weekly confrontations with our hecklers.

"At least we work and have some money," Peach shouted back at them.

"Look at those old clothes y'all got on," someone yelled out.

"At least we're gonna buy some new clothes! And you'll still be ugly," Evonne fired back.

This verbal exchange could go on for ten, fifteen minutes some Fridays. I just sat back and watched and listened, never uttering a word. It's funny…I never knew we were so poor until someone pointed it out. I always felt so loved and protected by my family that having so little money didn't really occur to me. Nor did it matter.

Chapter 11

HATERS GONNA HATE

It was fall. I reluctantly entered high school.

I was undergoing a metamorphosis of sorts. I'd hit a growth spurt. It seemed that overnight I had become a tall stick figure at about five foot eight, weighing about 115 pounds. I was shy and uncomfortable around other kids in part due to my strict upbringing and the watchful eye of my mom. My peers looked intimidating enough, and now I had to face bigger, more mature students, some of whom would just stare at me without uttering a word. I had also spent so much time with my siblings I found it difficult to make new friends.

High school was an interesting mix of kids trying to find themselves. There were about four hundred of us. Many struggled with trying to act grown-up, while others, like me, found comfort in just being a child. I didn't feel any pressure to grow up too fast, and besides, my mom's strict rules ensured there was no chance of that happening. I discovered in high school that most teenagers' parents were not nearly as strict as my mom. They had loosened the reins.

Academically, I found high school very rewarding. My teachers loved that I was never tardy, had perfect attendance, did my homework, earned good grades, and showed enthusiasm for learning. My social status was another story.

There were a lot of cliques: the pretty and popular girls, the wealthy girls, the girls who were putting out, and the nerdy, bookworm, awkward girls. I fell into the last category. Some pretty and popular girls who hung out after school were called the "Brick Houses" after the Commodores' 1977 hit single "Brick House." It was a huge compliment. If you were considered a brick house, it meant you had it all—the looks, the curves, the butt, the total package. And all the boys were attracted to you.

The wealthy girls in my high school had really nice clothes, some wearing a different outfit every day it seemed. Since I worked a summer job in the fields, my outfits were nicer, but I still wore my sisters' hand-me-downs. Mom always stressed the importance of taking care of the clothes we had because money was too tight to waste. My tall, skinny frame coupled with extreme shyness meant I sported a huge lack of confidence. I definitely was not a boy magnet. In fact, boys spoke to me mostly because I was known as one of the nice girls.

Still, I had a great friend—Gloria Cobbins. She and I were inseparable. I thought she was exceptional, and she had the whole package. She was average height with everything in all the right places: hips and lips, a shapely butt, and full breasts. She could turn heads with her confident walk, sassy style, and no-nonsense attitude. Gloria was one of the few girls who still sported an Afro, a hairstyle made popular in the 1960s consisting of large, coarse, African-American hair shaped roundly on the head. The Afro had played out, but Gloria still wore one, and it looked great. She also wore those huge hoop earrings. There was no money in Mom's budget for luxuries like jewelry, so Gloria let me borrow some of hers. I remember feeling kind of pretty in earrings.

At the end of my sophomore year, my appearance changed. I guess I began to blossom. I started to form quite a large chest in contrast to my small hips on my now five-foot-ten-inch frame. My hair grew long like my sisters' hair, and kids were starting to say I had pretty eyes. They always stared at the mole underneath my left eye. It became a conversation piece of sorts. Kids would ask, "Were you born with that mole under your eye?" or "Do you draw it on like some of the actresses?"

I was still so skinny that I didn't see myself as pretty, but some of the boys started to take notice.

* * * *

"This has to be an awful rumor," I said. "Why would someone want to fight me?"

"I heard it was because of Tiny," Gloria explained. "Her boyfriend told somebody he thinks you're beautiful."

Word had spread throughout school that I would be jumped and beaten by three of the popular girls during my lunch break.

"Beautiful?" I asked incredulously. I remember laughing. "I know that's not true."

"Well, maybe he said 'kind of cute,' but anyway, Tiny wants to beat you up. The word is, she hates you and says you think you're pretty."

"Pretty?" I replied. "Look at me. I mostly wear hand-me-downs that are too tight and too short. I'm lucky if my shoes fit, and I'm not allowed to wear makeup. The only jewelry I have is what you let me borrow. And that boyfriend of hers is a senior, and he only said hi to me. I have caught him staring a few times, but that's it."

"Well, that's the rumor," she said, looking worried. I was really scared now because Gloria looked so serious.

"When does she want to fight me?" I asked.

"Katie Mae, your sister Evonne's friend, told me Tiny, Georgia, and Donna are gonna jump you at recess tomorrow," Gloria said with certainty.

This was why students had started to gawk at me over the last few days. They knew about the fight tomorrow. Some looked as if they were chomping at the bit to see some action at our otherwise quiet school.

Tiny was a petite girl who always got compliments on her beautiful, black hair. She had a smooth, chocolate complexion. Her sister, Georgia, was almost the complete opposite—tall with a very light-skinned complexion. She was thick with a gorgeous body. So was Donna, although some thought she had a little too much backside. She flaunted her small waist and full hips and butt, wearing jeans so tight I was sure they would explode at the seams. They all garnered the boys' attention. They were quite the popular trio.

My anxiety and fear suddenly kicked in. I had never been in a fight. I had never bothered anyone. I had never even had so much as an argument with anyone. Mom always taught us to walk away from fights if we could. "If you can't, then defend yourself and whip their asses," she'd say.

"Thanks for telling me," I said to Gloria, looking concerned.

"What are you gonna do?"

"I don't know," I said, my head hanging low.

"Call in sick tomorrow," she whispered.

"I can't. Momma will ask what's wrong," I said, thinking about it, unsure if I should consider faking an illness.

"Tell her they gonna jump you." I remember Gloria grabbing my hands and covering them with hers. "I'm afraid for you, Romona, but you know I'll help you fight 'um."

"No, Gloria, I'll be fine," I said as if the life were being sucked out of my body. I couldn't stop worrying.

When the bell rang at the end of the day, I was so happy to see that Evonne had already boarded the school bus. I climbed in and sat next to her.

"Romona, what's wrong wit' you?" she asked, looking at me seriously.

I could never hide my feelings from Evonne. We were like twins. We told each other everything.

"They gonna fight me tomorrow during my lunch break," I said, trying to hold back my tears.

"Who gonna jump you?" she asked, spinning my shoulders around to look me straight in the eye.

"Gloria told me Tiny and Georgia and Donna gonna fight me during second-period recess when they know I'll be alone because *you* eat during third period, and they're afraid to fight me if you're around," I said, my eyes now watering.

"Romona, don't you cry. No one is gonna jump you," Evonne said, visibly angry. I hated to see that look in Evonne's eyes. When her family was threatened, she could morph into someone I didn't recognize, and it was frightening.

"What are you gonna do? We don't eat together. You'll be in class," I said.

"Don't you worry. Just go to school tomorrow, and after you eat lunch, walk outside like you always do," she said as if she had already hatched a plan.

"No!" I responded loudly, inches from her face. "If I stay in the cafeteria near some teachers until the bell rings, they won't hurt me. Shouldn't we just tell Momma? Or, I could tell Principal Bacchus."

"No, Romona! Don't I always look out for you?" she asked pointedly. "Don't I?"

"Yes, you do," I said with a big smile.

I loved Evonne. As a child, she had protected n from everything—stray dogs, bad dreams, cuddled with me when I was ill, or took the blame and faced Mom's wrath. But I was still terrified about tomorrow. How could she protect me if she wasn't around?

* * * *

When I heard our rooster crowing, I knew morning had come.

For the first time in my life, I dreaded going to school. I didn't have that usual, joyful pep in my step that made me spring out of bed and yell to my siblings it was time to go to school. Instead, I moved in slow motion. I hadn't slept well. I tossed and turned all night, wrestling with the feeling that I should tell Mom. I was scared. Actually, no…I was terrified.

I got up and went to Evonne's room, and I was surprised to find her looking great. She was chipper. She always wore her hair down, but this morning she tied her hair up and back, twisting it into a ball and pinning it tightly with bobby pins. She had also put on her black, two-inch, pointy-toed high heels that she never wore. Those were her Sunday shoes, strictly reserved to wear with dresses to church. Then she started filing those long nails of hers that she liked to keep pointed and sharp. No one had nails like Evonne. She would sometimes spend hours filing and polishing those things.

"Hey, Romona," she said with a huge grin as I stood in the doorway. "You ready for today?"

"No, Evonne. I don't wanna fight. I don't know how, but they gonna beat me up and we gonna get in trouble," I said nervously.

"Girl, I told you not to worry," she said, giving me a sheepish grin.

"You ain't scared for me?"

"Nah. Girl, it's gonna be all right," she said, still filing her nails. Those razor-sharp talons are to blame for some of the scratches still visible on my arm today. When she was mad at me, I never fought back. I did everything she told me to do.

As we walked to the bus stop, Evonne sang her favorite song:

Oh-hoh-hoh-hoah

Oh-hoh-hoh-hoah

Everybody was kung fu fighting. Huh!

Those kicks were fast as lightning. Huh!

In fact it was a little bit frightening

But they fought with expert timing…

Looking over at me, she said, "Come on, Romona. Dance and sing with me."

Evonne loved to dance when she heard that song. She and I and a few of the other dancers had formed our own soul train in music class before school. We competed to see who could come up with the most creative dance routines, and we danced to "Kung Fu Fighting" by Carl Douglas over and over again.

But I was in no mood to dance this morning. I couldn't even think. I was in a trance, filled with thoughts of the many ways I would be pummeled by three angry teenage girls. How could Evonne remain so calm? It was as if she knew something I didn't.

My lunch hour arrived. Second period. The crowd seemed noisier than usual. The atmosphere was thick with conversation, and many of the kids stared at me as I ate lunch with Gloria. I caught a glimpse of Tiny and her sidekicks. They appeared to be waiting for something, and I knew it was for me to finish lunch. I was taking an unusual amount of time, hoping to prolong the inevitable.

I thought about Evonne. *Why didn't she let me tell Momma? Maybe I should have told my favorite music teacher or the principal.* My mind raced with what-ifs. But Evonne had never let me down, so I did exactly what she told me to do.

As I got up to put my lunch tray away, Gloria asked, "Are you sure you don't want me to help you?"

"No," I whispered, fear in my eyes. "Evonne told me to just walk outside."

As I headed for the door, so did a lot of other kids huddled together like a herd of cattle. Outside, I couldn't believe it when they started to form a circle around me. It was like they were about to witness an Ali-Frazier prizefight. On one side, three tough teens. On the other side, me—a sad-looking soul who appeared to have just lost her puppy.

I saw them coming, all three of them. Some of the boys and girls laughed, as if they couldn't wait for a brawl. Other students looked on with sadness in their eyes, likely students who knew me and knew I would never hurt anyone.

Tiny was much shorter than me, but she got right up in my face. "So, you like my boyfriend, huh?" she shouted, so close to me I could smell her lunch on her breath.

"No, I don't, Tiny," I said. "I've never even talked to him."

"Just get her, kick her ass!" Georgia and Donna shouted.

Tiny stood inches away from me. I thought I had stopped breathing, when out of nowhere, Evonne appeared.

"Get away from my sister," Evonne screamed, violently pushing Tiny backward.

"What are you gonna do about it?" Tiny shouted back, walking a few inches toward Evonne, bringing them almost chest to chest. Georgia and Donna flanked Evonne. My heart raced. It had been beating three times its normal rate.

Suddenly, without any warning, Evonne pushed Tiny, and her fists started flying. Kids shouted, "Oh, it's on!"

Tiny tried to stretch her short arms to land a punch, but Evonne had the height advantage. The two of them weren't fighting with open fists; they were going at it like professional boxers. Evonne was getting the better of Tiny—punching her and pulling her hair—when suddenly she pulled Tiny's beautiful hair right off! We all looked on in disbelief. Her hair seemed to fall in slow motion, our eyes following its downward spiral to the ground.

The other kids laughed and pointed. "Tiny wears a wig!"

Tiny screamed, motioning for Evonne to wait a minute as she stopped to pick up her wig. Evonne stood there, looking perplexed, as we all were. Tiny had actually stopped the fight to pin her wig back on.

A few seconds later, she said, "Come on, Evonne!" and they picked up where they had left off. Evonne knocked her to the ground. Fearing Evonne was too much for Tiny to handle, Georgia and Donna grabbed Evonne from behind. I just stood there, torn between going to get help and trying to make them stop. The fight had only gone on for a few minutes, but it felt like so much longer.

Evonne held her own. She was fighting three girls and doing it well, but things turned ugly when one of Tiny's trio had Evonne by the waist, and two of them had her by the hair. By now I was shaking and rubbing my hands together, shouting, "Leave my sister alone!"

The boys and girls screamed at me. "Romona! Girl, you betta help yo' sister!" I didn't know what to do, so I did what came to mind. I reluctantly grabbed Donna. She was the biggest of the three, about five foot six and 130 pounds. I was taller than her but a twig compared with her full frame. I snatched Donna and swung her to the ground. I couldn't believe what little force it took. She fell like a rag doll. I don't even think I had to hit her.

Suddenly, a boy yelled, "Queen Kung Fu!" I looked up, still standing over Donna, and couldn't believe my eyes. Evonne was flying through the air, drop-kicking Tiny and Georgia. It looked like something out of a Bruce Lee film. *Where did she learn to fight like this?* I thought. The kids, whipped into a frenzy, cheered her on. The next thing I knew, several teachers grabbed our hands and pulled us apart. I knew I was in big trouble.

Some boys were still laughing and pointing at Tiny. I turned to see what was so funny. There was a much-disheveled Tiny, her wig on crooked, looking like a hot mess. No one had ever seen "Miss Perfect" look so out of sorts.

Tiny had blood on her face and hands, and she was screaming at Evonne and our teachers. "She hurt me!" she cried out.

"Tiny, how badly are you hurt?" one of the teachers asked as she searched Evonne's pants pockets for a knife. "What did you cut her with, Evonne?"

"Nothing," Evonne said.

"Tiny, what kind of weapon did she use on you?" the teacher asked.

"Her nails!" Tiny screamed. "She scratched my face with those sharp nails of hers."

"Romona, what are you doing?" another teacher asked as he grabbed my arm, looking at me in disbelief. He raised his voice. "You fighting?"

"I didn't want to," I said, feeling ashamed.

"I'm so disappointed in you. Come with me."

As I walked toward the door to the building with the teachers and the other girls, I heard some kids yelling, "It's not Romona's fault! They jumped her sister! She was just trying to break it up!"

I looked back at Evonne. I couldn't believe how pretty she still looked. She had already pinned her hair back up nicely without a brush or mirror. I was amazed even her heels hadn't come off.

We're definitely gonna be expelled from school, I thought as we followed the teachers into the principal's office. An even more frightening vision was Mom's wrath. Thoughts of how she might punish us infiltrated my mind. *Momma is gonna be furious.*

The five of us girls sat outside Principal Bacchus' office waiting for the teachers who had gone in to tell him what happened. Tiny had been bandaged up by the nurse. I felt bad for her, and I couldn't help but think how it had all started over insecurity about a boy.

"Come in, all of you," Principal Bacchus said, looking very angry. "Except for you, Romona." He stretched out his hand to stop me from entering. Instead, he pulled me aside. "Romona, when I heard five girls were involved in a fight, you were the last person who would have come to mind. Tell me what happened," he said in a surprisingly caring tone.

"Well, sir, Tiny, Georgia, and Donna wanted to fight me over a boy," I said. I was half out of breath and bursting with energy. I wanted to tell my side of the story so badly. "He's Tiny's boyfriend, and he's never even spoken to me, and I tried telling her," I said innocently. "But she kept saying she hated me for trying to steal her boyfriend, and it's just not true. Mr. Bacchus, I swear I've never even said two words to him."

"Why didn't you come to me, Romona? I would have protected you, and we could have avoided all of this," he said sincerely.

"I was scared to tell anyone, and I thought they'd just beat me up after school if I told. I didn't want to fight, Mr.

Bacchus, but they started to hurt my sister, all three of them." Tears were rolling down my face. "I just grabbed one of them and pulled her off my sister."

"I know, Romona. I believe you," he said. "You're a great student, but you should have come to me with this. You can go to class now," he said.

"Class?" I said, stunned. "I'm not suspended from school?"

"No," the principal said. "You've never been in trouble before, and the teachers say the other kids back up your story. You were just trying to break it up. Wipe those tears away and go on to class." With that, Principal Bacchus motioned for me to leave.

I was so worried about Evonne, though. I looked for her in the hallway as I went to my last class for the day, but I couldn't find her. I asked a few people, and no one had seen her.

Finally, the bell rang, signaling the end of the school day. I rushed to catch the bus home. I had to know what happened to Evonne. *Where is she?* I thought frantically. *What did they do to her?*

I rose up in my seat, looking out the window, trying desperately to find her in the crowd of students boarding the bus. My heart raced with fear. *Are they keeping her after school?* Katie Mae, who had told Gloria I would get beat up, took the seat beside me. She was out of breath, as if she were eager to tell me something. She was one of the school's gossip queens and always knew everything.

"I heard what happened to yo' sistah, Romona," she said, almost salivating because she wanted to tell me so badly.

"What happened?" I asked, grabbing her arm. "Where is she?"

"Girl, you didn't hear? Evonne, Tiny, Georgia, and Donna were all suspended for three days!" she shot back like a sly hyena that had gotten away with something. "Yo' mom had to come up to the school to get Evonne."

Oh my God, I thought. *Momma had to take off work to take Evonne home. We're in major trouble.*

When I walked in the front door, Mom and Evonne were in the living room waiting for me. So were a few of my other sisters. Mom was not happy. She had that look I never liked to see staring back at me.

"Romona!" she screamed, huffing and puffing.

"Yes, Momma?" I answered softly. My head hung slightly, but I looked up at her.

"Evonne tells me one of those girls hit you first and then she hit her. Is that true?"

It was Mom's rule that you never ever start a fight. You try to walk away unless someone hits you first, and then you give it all you've got. I knew Tiny hadn't hit me first, although she looked like she was going to. But I had never lied to Mom.

What do I say? I looked over at Evonne, who had the fear of God in her eyes. Seconds went by before I answered the question. Evonne was giving me the evil eye, as if to say, *You better save me from Momma's torment.* I knew Mom's punishment would be much worse than an expulsion from school. Not only would Evonne get a whipping with one of the switches from our maple tree in the front yard, but she wouldn't be allowed to come out of her room to eat, watch television, or make phone calls, and she would probably have to do everyone's chores for a month.

"Answer me, Romona!" Mom shouted. "Who hit first?" She stepped close to me and looked directly in my eyes. Evonne was still glaring at me, so I knew what I had to do.

"It was just like Evonne said, Momma. Tiny hit me first, and then Evonne hit her. They started the fight," I said.

"Okay, then. That's all I needed to know."

"Evonne, you were right to protect yo' sistah," she said, looking proud that Evonne had been courageous enough to take on three girls. I, however, felt awful. For the first time in my life, I looked my mom straight in the eye and lied to her. Even when Mom had asked if my pet pig, Missy, was in the house, I never lied; I just didn't answer. But this time, I had actually lied to her, and it didn't feel good.

"Thanks, Romona. I know you were scared," Evonne said later that night as we sat in her bedroom.

"No, thank you for saving me today," I smiled.

"Girl, you can fight!" I said excitedly. "You were spinning around like Wonder Woman. You had Linda Carter's superpowers and strength."

"Where did you learn karate?" I returned, laughing. "Who taught you how to drop-kick and fly in the air like that?"

"Girl, that was nothin'," she said coyly. "Nobody messes with my sistah. I'll always protect you, Romona," she said smiling, giving me a hug.

"I'm sorry you got suspended because of me, but how did you get out of class second period to come outside?" I asked.

"I told my teacher I had a stomachache and had to go see the nurse."

"Tiny really doesn't have much hair. Can you believe she wears a wig?" I said in an uncharacteristic moment of boastfulness.

"I know!" Evonne agreed. "Can you believe that?"

Chapter 12
IGNORE THE NAYSAYERS

Boys rarely tried to date me because our little white house at the end of the dirt road was aptly named "Valley of the Virgins." It was public knowledge around town that Mom was raising ten girls alone. The boys knew that Miss Henrietta's girls were off limits, and she kept a .22 caliber handgun in the house to ward off any potential suitors.

Of course, that was just a myth; the gun was for protection (though there wasn't much crime in our tiny town).

All through high school, Mom constantly drilled her mantra into our brains: "I've got ten girls, but I sho ain't gonna have ten grandbabies!" She meant it. She kept a tight leash on us girls. We didn't leave the house without asking for permission, and Mom had to know where we were going. She told us when we were expected back home, and there was a harsh price to pay if we weren't on time.

I did have a boyfriend toward the end of high school, but Mom never liked him because he didn't have career aspirations and didn't plan to go to college. He begged me not to go away to school. Instead, he shared his dreams of our marriage and him getting a job at the local gas station to take care of me.

But I wanted more. I tried persuading him to seek a college degree with me, but he insisted that if I went away our relationship might be over. I liked him a lot, but I loved the idea of college so much more. My appetite for a degree had grown, and the thought of becoming a journalist pulsated through my head.

After finishing my senior year early, I decided to go to a nearby technical school for a few months until graduation. I took up graphic arts and design. While there, I learned about newspaper writing, layout, and design and how to take still photos and develop them in a darkroom. During the summer, I took a job alongside my mom at the Brown Shoe Company, working on the assembly line to help pay my college tuition.

* * * *

Mom and I shared with others my dreams of becoming a television journalist, just like Mr. Cronkite. One Sunday, all of the high school seniors in my church had to stand up and announce their career aspirations to the congregation. I remember a few outbursts of laughter when I declared my career choice to everyone.

"She wants to do what and be like who?" Miss Salone said to Mom after services, walking fast to catch up with us before we made it to our car. Miss Salone, who was about sixty years old, was one of the "mothers" of the church.

I used to think Miss Salone and five or six of the other senior women in church were angels. After all, every Sunday they were decked out in white from head to toe: white dresses, white stockings, white shoes, white hats, white purses, and white gloves. I thought they had been sent from heaven by God to look after us. They even all sat together in church. I remember their hats used to block our view of the pulpit, so we tried not to sit behind them.

When I got older, Mom explained that, like the deacons, these women provided a much-needed service in the church. They oversaw church programs, providing their services free of charge. They did the cooking for our banquets, took care of the elderly and shut-in members of the congregation, and visited the sick in the hospital.

Miss Salone was a heavyset woman with salt-and-pepper hair. When she caught up to us, she pressed Mom about my career plans as if I weren't present.

"Henrietta, tell that guh to go up there to that college and majuh in somethin' sensible like nursin' or teachin' so she can get huh a job," she said as Mom and I stopped to listen to her.

"Sho nuff, Henrietta, she betta," another woman chimed in.

"They ain't gonna let poh black folk like us sit there next to those white people and read no news on television," Miss Salone said convincingly, as if she knew the people in charge of hiring broadcasters.

Mom just smiled and said, "Well, that's what she wanta do, and Romona can read good and gets good grades."

Walking away, talking loud for anyone to hear, Miss Salone cried, "Lawd, Lawd, Lawd, these chillins' are crazy! She gonna be like Walta Konkrite. What makes that chile thank she can be like Mr. Konkrite?" she went on. She always mispronounced Mr. Cronkite's name. I never corrected her because Mom always said not to talk back to your elders. It was disrespectful.

It was true; I had set my goals high. But Mom had taught me to pray for what I wanted and to work hard and have faith.

A few months later, I graduated high school, and I was on my way.

Chapter 13
COLLEGE BOUND

In 1977, I left home for the very first time.

I headed to Lincoln University for my freshman year of college. Lincoln was located in Jefferson City, Missouri's state capital. It was a five-hour drive northwest of my home. Lincoln was one of the oldest historically black colleges in the country. It was founded in 1866 by soldiers and officers in the 62nd Regiment of the United States Colored Infantry with support from the 65th Colored Infantry. When I attended, there were about 2,500 students.

I was intimidated and overwhelmed, but at the same time I was excited to go. Just to be on campus and know that black men fought in the Civil War and pooled their finances so kids like me might have a shot at a college education was truly awe-inspiring.

The dream I had had since I was six years old was finally coming true. "I'm in college," I whispered as if to remind myself. As I walked across campus, I was amazed by the four- and five-story buildings done up in red and brown brick. It was all so new to me; back home we didn't have buildings that big. I stopped in the middle of campus to take in my new surroundings. There were no fields, cows, or John Deere tractors in sight. In their place were students from all over the country, more kids than I'd ever seen before in my life—many more than the four hundred in my high school.

I felt so shy and awestruck that I became anxious and tense. Then I realized that I was missing Mom! I couldn't believe it. I always thought I'd be glad to grow up and leave home, but on my first day on campus, there was so much to take in that I became frightened. I wanted and needed my mom.

However, I knew God was watching. He was there with me. So, I snapped out of my trance and prepared for my first appointment to see Mr. Glasper, the head of the financial aid office. He was a tall, sophisticated man dressed in a nice suit and tie. He was clean-shaven, his shoes and belt matched, and he talked slightly differently than the people back home. In Wilson City, you didn't see many people dressed like he was unless you were going somewhere special.

When I arrived, though, he didn't look very happy to see me. Mr. Glasper strained a smile as he told me to come in and sit down. Right off, he hit me with news that was tough to swallow, telling me I was six hundred dollars short on my tuition. My Pell Grant couldn't be increased. He said he had already spoken with my mom. There was no way she could come up with the money. Work in the soybean fields had dried up shortly after my high school graduation, so there was no extra money to make up the difference. I had saved every penny I could working at the Brown Shoe Company, but we were still short.

"I have no choice but to send you home, Romona," he said, looking tortured as the words rolled off his lips.

I sat quietly and took a few seconds to digest what he said. Then I broke down right in front of him.

"Mr. Glasper, you don't understand. This is my dream. I have to go to college." I choked back tears as I spoke. "I'm begging you, please! Don't send me home!" I cried as if college meant life or death.

He suggested I go back home, get a job, and come back the next year when I had saved enough money. However, not only were there no jobs in Wilson City, but I couldn't go home. The embarrassment of having to go back and face all the naysayers was too much to bear.

I explained that I had told both God and Mom that I wanted to go to college since I was a kindergartner. He listened stoically as I poured my heart out, telling him how hard I had worked to get there. He looked at me with concern. "Romona, go to your dorm room. I'm going to help you work something out."

I prayed that night, telling God, *You told me I could go to college! Momma promised me my whole life I would get a college degree. For years I've lived a God-filled life. I can't make the long drive back to Wilson City. I'll be the laughing stock in my town, and my dreams will die there!*

When the sun rose the next day, I was already up, pacing my dorm room, waiting for Mr. Glasper to call. When the phone finally rang in the dorm's hallway, it was him. He told me he had been so impressed with my desire to stay in college that he found me a job working for my dorm mother in the office. It would pay just enough to cover the additional tuition costs.

I couldn't believe my ears. Mom was right; God could find a way out of no way. I knew Mr. Glasper was one of those gifts that Mom always said God places in your path.

Chapter 14

MY OWN HENRY HIGGINS

I loved Lincoln University; being on a college campus was amazing. I met so many interesting kids who hailed from New York to Texas to California, some of whom looked very different from the people I had grown up with. They sounded different, too. As I stood in the student union, I heard accents that were foreign to me. They must have thought my voice equally strange. A few people commented on my broken English, asking if I had been raised in the country. I wasn't offended, though. I was proud of my rural roots.

Even the way some of them wore their hair was unusual. I was used to my naturally thick, coarse hair that I pressed with a straightening iron once a week, but some of the black girls had long, straight hair. I wondered if they had been born with it that way. Others had gorgeous outfits I had only seen in catalogs and magazines. Many of them had nice shoes and purses to match.

Then there were the kids like me, the ones with no money who could barely afford college. It wasn't tough to spot us. We wore clothes a little too small or too big and borrowed books we couldn't afford to buy. We never had money to eat off campus, and we used every single drop of our personal hygiene products. Mom could only afford to send me a five-dollar monthly allowance, so I cut the plastic top off my lotion bottle and rubbed it dry. I used my bar of soap until it disintegrated in my hand. I shook my box of laundry detergent, using the dust to clean my clothes. But I was in college, and that was all that mattered to me. I wanted to earn a degree so badly.

* * * *

I declared my major in broadcast journalism. I loved my journalism classes the most. They were small, only about seven students in each class. We had some of the best professors, but one of my favorites was Dr. R. C. Wyatt. Dr. Wyatt was short in stature but big in personality and attitude. I believe he told us he was from England, which accounted for his thick foreign accent. He was an unusual-looking man—completely bald on top with fairly long, brownish-gray hair on the sides. He had big, bright, blue-green eyes and a neatly trimmed mustache and goatee.

Dr. Wyatt always wore a suit and tie to class. Sometimes his conservative suits looked a little too tight, and they restricted his movement. In any case, he ran his class as if he were a drill sergeant—walking with his head up and shoulders back, strictly formal when referring to us as "Mr." and "Miss." I don't think he ever called me "Romona." It was always "Miss Robinson."

Dr. Wyatt was excited about teaching. He was full of energy and constantly moving around, never sitting or standing in one place too long.

"Miss Robinson, you have a plethora of work to do!" he belted out before class one day.

"Plethora? What in the world does that mean?" I asked, eagerly awaiting his answer.

"Look it up!" he yelled back with a bold face. "All good journalists own dictionaries!"

He wasn't mean-spirited, just strict. He rarely smiled, careful to have his game face on at all times.

I really like this guy, I thought one day as I stared at him.

What I didn't appreciate, though, was how he quickly began ripping into my southeastern Missouri accent. At first, I was stunned and a little taken aback. I didn't think there was anything wrong with the way I spoke. But he told me harshly in front of the class that I'd never get a job if I continued to speak "broken" English. He was always on my case, stressing over and over that I read well, but I pronounced a lot of words incorrectly.

In my hometown, the adults had their own way of communicating. No one ever said it was incorrect. Instead of "door" it was "doh." Not "pork chops" but "pohk chops." "Forty dollars" was pronounced "fauty dollas." I inherited my Southern drawl from my mom, who was born in Arkansas, and from my grandparents, who were from Mississippi.

I had known Mr. Cronkite spoke differently than me. I assumed it was because he was a well-educated man and had gone to the best schools and colleges. But I learned from Dr. Wyatt that—unbelievably—Walter Cronkite was in fact born right up the road from me in St. Joseph, Missouri, only 440 miles from my house!

"Miss Robinson, I'm going to teach you to use proper English if it's the last thing I do," Dr. Wyatt informed me one day. "You have a lot of potential, young lady. I see it."

Dr. Wyatt made me his pet project. He put constant pressure on me in class, instructing me to get the local newspaper and read it in front of the mirror every night to practice my voice and diction. At first I felt a little silly, but night after night, I practiced in front of the mirror. It was much harder than I thought. Unless I concentrated on speaking well, I would drift right back into my old slang. One of the words I always butchered was "because." I don't ever remember saying that word before I got to college. We always said "'cause."

As the months went by, I started to hear the difference, and so did Dr. Wyatt. He walked around the classroom beaming with pride, telling me how amazed he was at the transformation. He had me read aloud in class, tapping my fingers with his pointer as I did. He hated how I pronounced the word "often." He cringed and gave me a tap every time I said "off-ten."

"The word is pronounced 'off-en,' Miss Robinson. The 't' is silent!" Dr. Wyatt was meticulous, constantly correcting me, and I could tell by the rare smile on his face when he looked directly at me that he loved every minute of it. I felt strange being singled out in class as if I were a science project to be dissected, tinkered with, and put back together. However, I must admit, I started to love the sound of my voice.

Dr. Wyatt also had me write articles for the campus newspaper, *The Clarion*, and I hosted a show on KLUM, the university radio station. My show, "Kaleidoscope," was an hour-long jazz program. At first, I did everything I could to avoid speaking since I was so self-conscious about my voice. But Dr. Wyatt would have none of it.

"Miss Robinson, I listened to your show this afternoon. Please say more than, 'You're listening to Kaleidoscope, I'm Romona,'" he admonished. "I'm bored stiff already, and it's only your second day on the air." Eventually, I became comfortable enough to read some public service announcements and a few news bulletins.

Even as I made progress with the help and encouragement of my family and college professors, I was still beset by my hometown naysayers telling me I could never become a journalist. I wasn't sure why the negative voices crept in. It was only when I didn't allow them a space in my head that I truly began to grow.

Chapter 15
NOT EVERYONE LIKES CHANGE

I remember the first summer I went home speaking differently. Evonne and her husband, Kevin, were home from his service in the Marines. Evonne had grown even prettier. Now with a newborn daughter whom she named after me, she flopped down beside me with little Romona on our living room sofa, getting right up in my face.

"Romona, girl, you sound proper and it sounds good! Say somethin' again," she said with a bright, energetic smile. "Kevin, come in here and listen to Romona talk," she yelled, motioning to her husband to hurry from the other room.

I was blushing. Everyone in the room stared at me. "Go ahead, read somethin', Romona," Evonne said. So I did. I sat there like a guinea pig, everyone smiling and listening intently as I spoke.

"Girl, you sound just like those people on the news, don't she, Momma? Romona, teach me how to speak like that, and pretend like you reportin' the news," Evonne said, now pulling on my arm.

"It's not hard to pronounce words correctly," I said to her with a childish grin, still feeling a little uncomfortable.

Later that day, Evonne and I walked down to the local community center. Some of the kids we had gone to school with were hanging around. I learned that not everyone liked the "new" way I spoke.

"What they been teachin' you up there at that white college?" one girl asked.

"It's a historically black college," I fired back.

"They teachin' huh how to talk like dem white people," another girl said.

Evonne quickly snapped back. "No, she's just learnin' how to talk proper." That was Evonne, still fighting my fights.

"I've been trying to learn to use the proper English," I chimed in. "If I'm gonna have a chance at being a broadcaster, my professors say I have to learn to speak correctly." I tried to sound humble so as not to offend them.

"Who says we don't talk right?" the girl asked. "Dem white people? Next thang we know, you gonna thank you betta than us."

The girls rolled their eyes at me in anger as they turned and walked away, making me feel as if I were not one of them anymore. *How can trying to improve myself garner such a negative response?* I wondered.

The next day, I attended church with my mom and family, and to my surprise, all of the reactions were positive. Reverend Tyus asked me to stand up and say a few words to the congregation. This was routine for kids returning home, no matter where they had been. I stood and told the members of the church how good it felt to be home and how thankful I was for the opportunity to go to college. As I continued to talk, I noticed Mom was looking up at me with such pride, and so were the mothers of the church, still decked out in white. I spotted Miss Salone whispering to one of the other mothers. I would give anything to know what she was saying about me.

* * * *

As I packed my things to head back to school, the negative fallout of my new speech plagued me. *Why can't I just concentrate on the positive responses and feel good about how far I've come? After all my months of hard work, why do I feel like an outsider around the people I've grown up with?*

But it didn't take long for my common sense to kick in, the common sense Mom said God had given me. *I can't please everyone, and why should I try? I am trying to do something positive with my life. If some people don't like it, maybe it says more about them than me. I am not going to let negativity trap my progress.*

After all, I had a goal to reach, and I needed to concentrate on the path to get me there.

Chapter 16

WELCOME TO THE WORKFORCE

After four years at Lincoln, in 1981, I achieved my dream. I became the fourth college graduate in my family. It was one of the proudest moments of my life.

I felt my professors had prepared me to take the next step toward my career—to go out into the world and get a job. I was armed with knowledge, something no one could ever take away from me. I imagined that landing a great job came swiftly after working hard in college, getting good grades, and graduating. I was ready.

But it wasn't that easy. I went on interview after interview, and no one hired me. Jefferson City was a small town, so my options in television and radio were few. The responses from TV news and radio music directors were disheartening:

"You have no experience. Go back to school."

"Your voice is awful. You're not ready."

"You should consider graduate school. You're not ready for television."

After about fifteen interviews, inside and outside my field, I was completely discouraged. But my faith and my family would not let me give up. I had worked so hard to become a broadcaster, and I was not about to throw in the towel just yet.

I finally decided to try my luck at a country radio station in Jefferson City. I was warned that KLIK 95 Country didn't hire blacks, but I would never let perceived racism prevent me from finding work. Of course, I knew nothing about country music. I had grown up listening to Motown, R&B, and gospel. But there I sat in the station manager's office, and when he told me I was hired, I was stunned. I would be a disc jockey, working the graveyard shift from 10:00 p.m. to 6:00 a.m.

It was a low-paying job—only four dollars an hour—but it was a job nonetheless. However, my jubilation turned to anxiety when I did the math. *How am I going to survive on thirty-two dollars a day?* I wondered. Apartments weren't cheap, and I would need a car to drive to work. My sister, Beulah, had loaned me her car just so I could go to interviews. I would also have to feed and clothe myself.

I guess I had assumed that after four years of college I would make a lot of money—at least $50,000 in my first job. Come to think of it, I had been so focused on my dream I never even asked how much broadcasters made. I just figured they were paid well.

I drove back to Beulah's house, where I had been staying since graduation. Worry filled my mind, but Beulah, the first in our family to graduate college, quickly put me at ease. She had become a teacher, and her husband, Oliver, was a state highway patrolman. They allowed me to stay with them until I could afford to live on my own. Oliver even let me borrow his old car for a few months until I was able to buy my first car—my pride and joy, a used 1980 Mustang II.

The excitement that remained of my new job dissipated after only a few days at the station. Not everyone there was happy to see me. I believe I was their first black on-air personality. The only other female deejay was nice to me, but it was a nervous kindness, as if she were afraid to be seen being too kind or too helpful. Two of the white male hosts were a different story. Their long hair and beards seemed to swallow their faces. They always wore plaid flannel shirts, and I don't think they ever smiled, at least not at me. The radio station was small, dark, and cramped. I remember there was a swinging door going into the radio booth. One day, I was walking closely behind one of the male hosts, thinking he would hold the door for me, but instead, he let it swing back, and it nearly slapped me in the face. I suppose I knew how he felt about me at that point if I didn't already.

Growing up, I had only gotten a small taste of bigotry and racism when our schools were first integrated, so I was shocked at how these adults were behaving in the workplace. One day, still trying hard to fit in, I joined a conversation the other deejays were having about their pets. I made the mistake of telling them I was afraid of stray cats. It was a phobia I had developed on the farm where vicious strays chased me and scratched me if they got close enough.

I left work one morning when it was still dark. As I approached my car, I was mortified. About two dozen eggs were splattered all over the roof of my Mustang, and the largest cat I'd ever seen sat atop the car, devouring them. I let out a scream, but of course, no one came running to my aid. Thankfully, I had startled the cat, and it scurried away.

As I drove home with dried egg all over my car, I asked God, "Why don't they like me?" I prayed intently, remembering how hard I had worked to get to this point, and I asked God to please protect me.

I walked into the station the next day with a smile on my face, and I never mentioned the incident. I wasn't sure who was to blame—likely the two bearded personalities who didn't look at me or speak to me that day—but I was afraid to complain after only a few months on the job, so I just let it go.

Chapter 17
THE DREAM IS ALIVE

A few months later, one of the local television stations had an opening for a reporter. A former college classmate who was interning at KRCG, the CBS affiliate in Jefferson City, told me I should send in my résumé and radio audition tape. I wasted no time getting one of my radio air checks to the news director. I think I stopped breathing for a moment when he called me a few days later for an interview.

When I arrived at the station, another candidate was there, too—a thin, attractive woman of average height with very nice teeth. She said she was a weekend television reporter in Philadelphia. I was immediately intimidated. I was just a few months out of college with hardly any radio experience and zero TV experience. I couldn't help but wonder why someone from such a big television market—the third largest in the country—would want the job. Jefferson City was small-market television, 145th in the country at the time, I believe.

Overcome with curiosity, I asked why she was leaving Philly. She told me her husband received a promotion in town, and she planned to move to Jefferson City with him. The more I looked at her, the more I thought I was way out of my league. This woman had it together. She had flawless, vanilla-colored skin and beautifully coiffed hair. Her suit looked expensive, unlike anything I had ever seen. I still recall the incredible shine on her black, patent leather shoes.

I glanced down at my own clothes. My yellow cotton shirt was stiff because I had loaded it with starch, and I accessorized it with a huge, blue scarf, equally stiff, tied into a humongous bow around my neck. The scarf matched my navy skirt, but my blue shoes had scuff marks, and they were a different shade of blue entirely. My hair and makeup could never compete with hers. Suddenly, I was struck by the fear that my wardrobe was a recipe for disaster. Money was tight, so I didn't have much to spend on clothing.

Just as I was about to dart home to change, the door opened, and the Philly reporter was called in for her interview.

"Good luck," I said to her.

"Thank you," she said, looking back at me with a cool confidence.

I sat there panicking for another thirty or forty minutes, going over in my head what I would say in the interview. I posed questions to myself aloud, pretending to be the interviewer, and then I answered my own questions. The secretary glanced up a few times and smiled. I guess she could see how anxious I was.

I thought of faking an emergency and asking the secretary if I could reschedule, thinking that when the news director went from seeing the Philly reporter to taking one look at me, it would be over. But a voice in my head kept saying, "You're as close as you'll ever be to realizing your dream, so stop it!" That had to be Mom's voice. Maybe Beulah's. God had never spoken to me that way.

My heart pounded as the door opened again. The Philadelphia reporter walked out and smiled at me as the secretary motioned for me to go in. I was terrified. A thousand thoughts rushed through my brain at once. I tried to remember all of the lessons I had learned about job interviewing at college. I had flashbacks of Dr. Wyatt with his pointer: *Speak up, Miss Robinson! Speak clearly and concisely! Enunciate, Miss Robinson! Hold your head up!*

"Have a seat, Romona," the news director said. "I've listened to your work on KLIK, and it's not bad." I was silent for a second. This was one of the news directors with whom I had previously interviewed, someone who told me my voice needed work and that I wasn't ready for TV.

"I work the graveyard shift. I'm surprised you're up so early to listen," I replied.

"It's my favorite radio station. I turn it on every morning at five thirty, and I get to hear the end of your show."

His face is a blur now, but I can still feel his intimidating presence when I think back to that day.

"I can hear you have been working on your voice," he continued. "It's gotten better in a short time. Did you write your own news stories for newsbreaks and commercials and jingles?"

"Yes," I said, swallowing quickly to try and wet my mouth, fearing I had a frog in my throat. My right leg swayed from side to side. It was something I did when I was nervous. I could envision Mom motioning for me to stop like she did on Sunday mornings when I sang in our church choir as a kid. The leg could take on a life of its own when I was in panic mode. Thankfully, he couldn't see my leg over his desk.

"Romona, I'm still concerned that you have no television experience. A part of me feels I would be taking a huge gamble hiring you." I didn't know if it was a statement or a question.

After an awkward silence, I answered, "No, you wouldn't."

Oh no! I sat stone-faced for a moment. *One- or two-word answers are not good if you want to work in television,* I thought. But I was so nervous.

"Romona, why should I hire you with no television experience?" he asked.

Yes! This is the question I've been preparing for. I know this answer.

I paused a moment, looked him directly in the eye, and said, "Because I know this city. I've spent four years in college here, and I love its people. I understand their needs and wants and struggles."

The latter part of the statement wasn't quite true. I had been busy at college and work the last few years to know that, but it sounded good at the time. What *was* true was what I said next: "I believe I have all the ingredients to become an aggressive, solid reporter. I have a broadcast journalism degree, and in my short tenure at the radio station, I've been given important assignments to write, produce, and deliver several newsbreaks and jingles every day. I have done these under tight deadlines, which forces me to think on my feet and decide which of several stories are newsworthy and condense them into a one-minute script. There is a lot of fast-paced, creative writing expected of me, and I meet those challenges consistently. I've learned so much in a short period of time."

"Like what?" he asked, leaning over his desk as if he were hanging on my every word.

"I have learned to check and double-check the facts to make sure my stories are confirmed before airing them. Even though I've never done on-air television work, I think my writing is my strongest asset."

The news director was now sitting up, almost nodding his head as I spoke. I took this as a good sign.

"Sir, I'm eager to learn and grow as a journalist. If you hire me, I will work hard to prove you weren't wrong to take a chance on me with no TV experience. I can work day or night or weekends. I'm available to start now. You will not regret your decision."

He asked me to go back to the lobby until he called for me again. I waited nervously. I wasn't sure what to make of this. It was the first interview at which I had been asked to wait.

What does this mean? They didn't ask the woman from Philadelphia to stay.

Fifteen minutes later, I was called back into the office. Before I could take my seat, the news director said, "Congratulations, Romona. You've got the job."

I couldn't believe my ears. I think I even said something really dumb, like, "Really? Why?"

"Romona, I see a lot of potential in you. While you don't have any television experience, I see a fire in your eyes and a thirst to learn and work hard. It's the kind of hunger and determination that can take you far in this business. Plus, you're local, a hometown girl. You know the city, and you have a look I think will appeal to our viewers."

I looked down at my wardrobe, unsure whether it was a joke about the horrendous outfit I was wearing. Maybe it was a good thing I couldn't afford expensive clothes. I looked more like a girl from Missouri's heartland. But then again, the on-air anchors and reporters in the heartland of Missouri tended to wear flannel shirts and khaki pants.

I shook his hand and said thank you. I couldn't believe it. I had just landed my first job as a television reporter.

As I drove back to my sister's house, I screamed at the top of my lungs, thanking God. I pounded my hands on the steering wheel and shook my head. "I'm a television reporter! I did it! I've got to call my mother, my sisters, and everyone I know!" I shouted, not caring that the other motorists looked over at me, puzzled by my wildly animated gestures.

Once I calmed down, my mind drifted back to my childhood and Miss Salone that one Sunday after church. Her words reverberated in my head: "They ain't gonna let poh black folk like us read no news on television." She was wrong. I was a television reporter, hired by a white person, and I was about to become a journalist working alongside white people.

Chapter 18
OPPORTUNITY KNOCKS

My first few months on the job in 1982 at KRCG-TV13 were exciting. I had told the news director I was willing to work hard, and did I ever. I hit the ground running, learning as much as I could as fast as I could.

On an average workday, reporters would shoot their own stories, which included interviews, video to support the story, and stand-ups. Stand-ups are when you see a reporter on camera during the story, usually providing an important nugget of information. When we got back to the station, we did our own writing, voice track, and editing. We called it a "one-man band."

All of the reporters worked alone for the most part unless it was a big story. Then we would double up. But we didn't have many big, breaking news stories in the quiet capital of Missouri.

* * * *

In the beginning, I had a partner reporter, Dan Dietrich, who trained me on shooting and editing. He was a tall, sandy-blonde-haired handsome guy with a lot of experience in the business. Every day was a new adventure. We covered everything from interviews with Missouri Governor Kit Bond to bake sales. Dan and I were a great team.

In just a few weeks, he gave me an entire crash course in broadcast news. All through college, I was taught that the top priorities in broadcast journalism were fact collection, clear and concise speech, credibility, objectivity, and believability. Dan taught me that, while those things were crucial, the three most important things in television reporting were writing, writing, and writing. "Never underestimate it," he said. "If you can write, you'll always have a job."

Dan made learning on the job fun. He was generous, continually sharing different ways I could be creative in my writing and reporting. He advised me to subscribe to at least three newspapers so I would know what was going on in the city, the state, the nation, and the world.

Dan joked with me when I couldn't hold the camera steady on my shoulders or when the video I shot was out of focus, but—as good an anchor and reporter as he was—the truth is he wasn't so great at teaching me the basics of operating the camera. Even after months of Dan spoon-feeding me instructions on how to shoot video, I still wasn't getting the hang of it. I found it extremely difficult to keep the ten-pound camera steady on one shoulder with the fifteen-pound deck and power pack on the other while keeping myself steady. I also had to remember to white balance the camera first to make sure the color was correct. It was all so confusing.

Week after week, I came back to the station with blue video because I had forgotten to white balance the camera or a shaky picture because I couldn't keep the camera steady. About four months later, I was summoned to the news director's office. I was certain I was going to be fired.

"Romona, you're just not cutting it as a photographer," he said in a solemn tone. "Every day you bring back pictures not quite suitable for television."

Fearing this was the end, I interrupted to ask for a little more time, assuring him the pictures would get better, but he wouldn't hear of it, and what he said next left me totally astonished.

"How would you like to try your hand at anchoring this weekend?" he asked.

I was so stunned that I actually said no. "Anchor? I can't do that," I said.

"Don't you want to think about it?"

"I don't have to. I'm not ready," I said as I left his office, thanking him for the opportunity. I ran to call Beulah.

* * * *

Beulah was one tough sister. She was the first person in our family to go to college and one of the first in our small town to ever get a degree. She was short, but she stood tall and confident in every aspect of her life. She always knew what she wanted. She was a go-getter, determined to achieve her goals—and she did. She had majored in education and loved her job as a schoolteacher in Jefferson City. As an educator, she hated the words "I can't." She was strong and ambitious and believed anyone could do anything they wanted in life so long as they applied themselves and were willing to acquire the education.

When I called Beulah to share the news about the offer to anchor, I forgot about her no-nonsense attitude.

"Oh my goodness, Beulah, he wants me to anchor this weekend. He wants me to sit in that chair and anchor a newscast. Of course, I told him there's no way. I can't do it. I'm not ready."

I waited for her to agree, but there was dead silence on the other end of the phone.

"What did you just say you said to him?" Beulah asked, puffing in the way she always did when she got agitated. Before I could even reply, she went on. "You said the words 'I can't' and 'no way'? Is that what you just said to me?"

"It's so sudden, Beulah," I said in a softer tone. "One minute I thought he was going to fire me and the next he's offering me a chance to anchor. I've never anchored a newscast, and thousands of people will be watching me make a fool of myself if I don't do well. I didn't know what else to say to him, so I said no."

My voice was getting hoarse as I rambled because I was so nervous. I could tell Beulah wasn't pleased with me. Without hesitation, she shot back at me in a stern, authoritative voice. "You can and you will anchor this weekend, Romona!"

She sounded very much like Mom. Beulah was always like a second mother to us. As one of the oldest sisters, she had been in charge of babysitting when Mom wasn't home. So, like a child being scolded, I replied, "Okay, Beulah."

I went back to the news director and told him I had changed my mind; I would fill in for the vacationing weekend anchor.

* * * *

It was a few days before my weekend debut. I was in a zombie-like state the whole time.

News travels fast in a small town. Not only was the station abuzz with the news that I would be filling in, but Beulah had also told everyone at her school that her little sister was going to be anchoring for the first time and that they had to watch at 10:00 p.m. Word spread to my professors at Lincoln, and then to the students, that a Lincoln alumnus would be anchoring the weekend news.

Of course, I was besieged by indecision and thoughts of failure and fear. *Should I buy a new outfit? A suit? A dress? Or should I look plain and simple? Should I wear my hair up or down? Pulled back or with bangs? What should I do with my hands while I'm on set? Will I be the laughing stock of the city? What will my professors think? Will I let down my news director who is taking a huge risk?*

But then there was Beulah. She encouraged me and lifted me up, telling me I was good enough and that I could do this. I practiced reading the daily paper in my mirror at home every night. I walked around the house talking to myself, remembering this was what I had been dreaming about since I was a girl. Finally, I convinced myself to take it all in, take a deep breath, and savor the moment.

Chapter 19

LIGHTS, CAMERA, AND NOT MUCH ACTION

Finally, the day arrived. It was a Saturday in 1983. I was done wrestling with my wardrobe. I eventually settled on the yellow-and-blue outfit, the same one I had worn when I was hired. I wore it to church once, and someone commented that I looked like such a "professional lady," so it seemed like good luck.

I wasn't expected into work until 2:30 p.m. for the 10:00 p.m. broadcast, but I showed up at 11:30 a.m. I convinced myself that my daily ten-minute drive could become three hours if there was an accident on the one-lane road. I also thought I needed to get in and start preparing for the show just in case there was breaking news.

I walked through the doors of the station. It was a ghost town. There was not another body in sight. I did find an engineer in the control room, but he looked too busy to notice I was there. I made my way down the hall to the newsroom. It was pitch dark, completely empty—no manager, no assignment editor, no producer, no reporter, no one. It's not like I was expecting anyone. The weekends were a skeleton crew. It would include the meteorologist, one studio camera operator, and me. I would be in charge of any reporting, producing, writing, editing any tape, running the assignment desk, taking viewer calls, running my own prompter, and anchoring the news and sports.

The loud, clattering sound of the AP machine was a welcome relief. The sound meant the machine was working and that the Associated Press wire was feeding and printing important news stories from around the world—critical information I would need to help produce the newscast later that night.

I flipped the light switch and plopped down into my gray swivel chair to cozy up to my desk. The smell of my fried ham sandwich I brought for dinner permeated the brown paper bag I placed next to my typewriter. There would be no time to go out and get dinner; after all, I could be hit by a car and miss my debut. So, I made sure I had my favorites: fried ham smothered in mayonnaise sandwiched between two slices of white bread, a honey bun, and a bottle of Coca-Cola.

I grabbed a white piece of paper, inserted it around the roller in my typewriter, and tapped a few keys to make sure it was functioning properly. I had to be certain there was enough ink and that all of the machines operated properly when I needed to start writing scripts for the show.

Then I just sat there, tapping and twisting left and right, glancing up at the caramel-colored walls, having visions of everything and nothing at all. I glanced at the huge "TV13 NEWSROOM" letters that hung on the wall as a backdrop to the set. They were done in a bold, brown font. "TV13" was enclosed in the CBS eye logo. My eyes wandered toward the front of the newsroom, and the set in the studio came into view. A wall of glass and a glass door separated it from the newsroom.

Curiosity got the better of me as I pushed open the door into darkness. I didn't want to bother the only engineer to turn on the massive overhead lights for me. Besides, the lights from the newsroom provided just enough brightness to explore. I could see the cream-colored plastic chair with a faux-leather orange front that I would sit in. It was important that I make sure the seat was suitable. It needed to be high enough and not have any screws loose. I placed my hands on the matching, cream-colored, faux-wood desk with a faux-Maplewood front and glided into my chair, rolling it back and forth and side to side. Comfort was paramount.

As the hours inched closer to my debut, I sought comfort in my dinner. The smell of my fried ham sandwich produced precious memories of my childhood—the fresh ham we ate from our farm animals and snuggling next to Mom to watch my idol. It was painful to reconcile her absence in my brain. I felt the enormity of what was about to happen, and I wanted and needed my mom. No long distance phone calls were allowed in the newsroom, and there were no cell phones back then, so it was just my tangled thoughts and me. To calm myself, I perused my mental catalog of her teachings. She always said we were on a dirt road to somewhere. *Momma,* I thought, *I have finally arrived at my planned destination.*

After I ate, I wrote a few stories, and then I turned and twisted in my chair for hours, only getting up to stretch my legs. It was 9:40 p.m. My steps were small and my breathing labored as I walked into a now well-lit studio minutes before I was to go on. I said hello to the camera operator, and he wished me luck, saying I'd be fine. It was no comfort. I quickly prayed to God, asking Him to help me. I did nothing without praying first.

My knees felt like they would give out from under me, just as I had felt on the day I was baptized. I was surprised by a little perspiration on my forehead since the studio was kept at a chilled sixty degrees due to the equipment and hot overhead lights. I looked down to make sure I was carrying my powder. I knew it would be essential to blot out any visible signs of stress. Even my hands felt clammy. As I strode toward the anchor's chair, it was as if time stood still. I felt like I was the only person moving. I sat down and looked up at the dozens of lights beaming down on me. My right leg violently swung back and forth. I massaged it vigorously, which usually produced calm.

As I examined the teleprompter and glanced at my scripts, my mind drifted back to my childhood again—how I had loved reading the words off the television screen, my sisters yelling for me to be quiet. But they weren't with me now. I was all alone.

This is what you've always wanted, I told myself. *You wanted to be a journalist—an anchor—like Walter Cronkite. This is it. This is your dream.*

I had prayed to God this day might come. I wanted to stop right there in my chair and start praising Him again, but I couldn't. In a matter of minutes, I would be anchoring my first live newscast.

The first words on the teleprompter read, "Good evening. I'm Romona Robinson." I practiced them over and over. I was pretty sure I could say my name, but I wanted to be certain because I felt like I was having an out-of-body experience, like it really wasn't me, yet it was. As the news open began to roll, I heard the taped announcer's voice say, "This is KRCG News!"

The moment had arrived. It was time to perform.

Blood rushed to my head as I read. Like a high-performance engine, I went from zero to sixty in a matter of seconds, reading for dear life. I can't recall the stories from that night, but I do remember that I read them at record speeds. I wasn't smiling, and I hardly looked into the camera, just down at my script. I got lost several times and fumbled the words as I tried to find my place on the teleprompter.

I showed no emotion. Even when I was reading a lighthearted story, my face was frozen. I had read and reread my scripts ten times, yet I butchered easy words. The bass in my voice escaped me, and my delivery was more like that of a high-pitched little girl. I thought, *If I can just get through the first eleven minutes, then we'll go to commercial break, and I can regroup before weather. Just get through eleven minutes.*

I was relieved when it was time for the weather. Cindy Whistler was our weekend meteorologist. She had a wonderful personality and always wore a big smile. When I looked at her on the two-shot, barely managing the words, "It's time for weather," she jumped right in and said, "Romona, it's good to have you with us this weekend." She made me feel so comfortable. For a moment, I forgot I was on television, and the usual small talk going into weather felt natural.

As I said goodnight to the audience, it took a minute before I could rise from my chair. The weight of the moment had finally hit me—what had just happened and what I had accomplished.

"Great job, Romona," Cindy said smiling, giving me a quick hug. "How does it feel to get the first one under your belt?" she asked.

"That was terrifying and horrible," I said, fishing for some encouragement. I had loosened up a bit by the end of the show, but I was pretty sure my performance had been a disaster.

"Naw, you were fine. Just a few nerves, but it's your first newscast," she politely responded.

The camera operator had come by the desk to congratulate me and to say goodnight. "Do you think you'll come back tomorrow?" he jokingly asked. I knew it meant my performance was pretty bad.

As it turned out, it wasn't as bad as I thought. Shortly after making my debut, I was offered the job of weekend anchor. I was told a few viewers had called in with positive comments, saying they thought I was sweet. If there were any negative comments, my bosses had the good sense not to share them with me.

Soon I started getting a lot of fan mail from local prison inmates. For a relatively small town, Jefferson City had four prisons. Even if my fans were criminals, they sure helped boost my confidence with their encouraging words. Some of the letters were pleas for dates once they were released, but many who had been incarcerated for years expressed happiness at finally seeing a black woman anchoring the news in the '80s. They encouraged me to continue representing the community. Thinking back, some of their letters were so well written and professional, it made me question how and why talent like that ended up in jail.

Chapter 20
MR. PRESIDENT

As much as I enjoyed anchoring the news, I really loved hitting the streets as a reporter. I worked hard and landed some plum assignments.

One of my most memorable assignments was covering the president of the United States, Ronald Reagan, in August 1984. He was scheduled to visit nearby Sedalia for a campaign stop to court Missouri farmers. This was a huge story for me. I couldn't believe the station was entrusting a young reporter to cover such a momentous event.

As my fellow reporter, Kermit Miller, and I got into position inside the venue at the Missouri State Fairgrounds, President Reagan emerged from a side door and walked to the podium. Just as I had always imagined, the White House press corps was there with him. They were all impeccably attired in their tailored suits. I glanced at my red-and-white polyester dress, purchased from J.C. Penney for about thirty dollars. I suddenly felt inadequate, but the excitement of getting a great story quickly put those thoughts out of my head.

The president lit up the room—the way he walked, his perfectly coiffed hair, and the big smile he flashed at his supporters. The energy in the room was electric. *Is this a presidential campaign speech on agricultural policy or a rock concert?* I thought. The raucous crowd made it difficult to tell.

As the cameras flashed, I snapped back to reality. I had the lead story covering the president of the United States, and I didn't want to mess it up. I had to forget about his Hollywood good looks and charisma. I needed objectivity and clarity about his remarks.

The rest of that day is a bit of a blur, likely the result of my adrenalin mixed with awe, but I do remember that covering President Reagan's visit helped bolster my confidence and faith in myself. For the first time in my short career, I felt that if I could cover the president, no assignment was too big for me to handle.

Chapter 21

OCCUPATIONAL HAZARD

One day, I was assigned to interview a wildlife photographer from *National Geographic*. He had a unique way of photographing wild animals. He would bring them to his farm, study their habits, and capture their behavior on camera.

When I arrived with my cameraman, the photographer was waiting for us outside an electrified fence. Behind it was a seven-foot-tall, five-hundred-pound black bear.

I looked at the photographer—a man of medium build with a graying beard who greeted me warmly and didn't look crazy. But he'd have to be to bring wild wolves and bears to his home, trust them, and get close to them.

"Why the electrified fence?" I asked.

"It's a security measure to make sure the animals don't escape. They all wear collars, and if they try to climb over the fence, they'll get a shock," he explained.

He invited my cameraman and me to come inside the fence. I was apprehensive at first, as there was a large and intimidating bear. When he stood on his hind legs, he was massive. By the looks of his jaws, he could probably fit my entire head in his mouth. His claws were like meat hooks, only much thicker.

"I know he's huge, but he's harmless," the photographer assured me. "And look, he loves Milk Duds." He held out some Milk Duds to demonstrate how the beast ate them out of his hand. He convinced me to try it. To my surprise, the bear was a gentle giant. His fat tongue lapped the candy from the palm of my hand. I could feel his hot breath as he rolled the chocolate goodies into his gaping mouth. *He sure does have big teeth,* I thought.

"I assure you, it's safe to come behind the fence," said the photographer.

Somewhat reluctantly, I agreed. When I looked back at my cameraman, he shook his head. "No way am I coming in there, Romona. I'll shoot from outside the fence," he said.

"Okay, scaredy-cat," I shot back as I entered the cage. I watched as the photographer snapped pictures. He positioned the bear's giant paws on a tree trunk for one photo and had him stand and raise both paws for another. It was captivating. I had never been so close to a bear in my life.

After we got enough video for the story, it was time for my interview. From the other side of the fence, my cameraman handed me the microphone. "We're rolling!" he announced.

I felt so at ease I actually forgot the bear was right there. A few minutes later, though, a huge roar interrupted the interview. It was a deep, screeching sound unlike anything I had ever heard. At that moment, I felt something clamp down on my right calf. I couldn't look down; I knew exactly what it was. Without hesitation, I ran for my life. I was breathing heavily, but surprisingly, I wasn't screaming.

What luck that I wore a dress and high heels that day. When you work as a general assignment reporter in television, you never know where you will be going the next day. Had I known about *this* assignment, I would have dressed differently.

My high heels sank into the grass as I sprinted, slowing me down. I could see a tree about twenty yards ahead. I turned to look, and the bear was right behind me, gaining on me quickly. I knew that if it caught up to me it would pounce on me like a cat on a mouse.

Everything happened so quickly. The photographer grabbed a whip, and he chased the bear, trying to head him off, but he only had eyes for me. I could hear the sound of the bear grunting, his heavy paws pounding the ground behind me.

I reached the tree, only to discover the nearest branch was fifteen feet high. There was no way I could climb it. I was too terrified to turn around; I could swear the beast was on the nape of my neck. I was breathing heavily and scared to death. I did the only thing I could think of—hide behind the tree.

I didn't know a bear could move so fast! This is it! I'm going to be eaten alive!

When I quickly peeped out from behind the tree, I was face-to-face with the bear. He stood on its hind legs and let out another long roar.

If this were a movie, this would be the moment when the woman faints, but it was real, and I had the starring role. Suddenly, the photographer whipped the bear, yelling, "Get away from her, get away from her."

Finally, the bear turned and lumbered off in the opposite direction.

All I could say was, "Oh my God! Thank you, Jesus!"

When I finally regained my composure, I looked down to check out my leg. The bear had bitten my calf, piercing the skin from one side to the other. I thanked God. If the bear had bitten down harder, he would have taken off my entire leg.

Then I turned my attention to my cameraman. He had never put down the camera to try and help me. He had kept rolling, capturing the entire incident on video. I gave him the evil eye at first, but as we stared at one another, we let out a belly laugh.

"I told you not to go inside that fence," he said. I knew he was right, but when you're a young reporter trying to make a name for yourself, I guess it brings out the daredevil in you.

He took the footage back to the station, but I figured there would be no story that day. My boss told me to see a doctor right away. I got a clean bill of health—it was just a small puncture wound—and was sent home, still shaken by the experience.

I arrived home shortly before the six o'clock evening newscast. When I flipped on the television, I was stunned to hear the anchors saying, "Coming up tonight, our own Romona Robinson is attacked by a bear!"

Surely they're not going to show me running for my life in high heels and a dress.

But that's exactly what they did. They showed all five foot ten of me looking like a deer in headlights as I ran away from a huge bear. It was not one of my finest TV moments, but as it turned out, it was one of the highest-rated newscasts that month.

It took me months to live down the embarrassment. No matter where I went in town, I was known as the "bear girl." Mom wasn't laughing, though. She made me promise I would never do something so foolish again.

Romona's first anchor job, KRCG-TV 1983

House I grew up in

Henrietta Robinson — mother

Romona & sister Brenette after working in the fields

Romona (front) Evonne (left) and Brenette (right)

Evonne Robinson — sister

Romona & sister Beulah

Chapter 22
INSIDE PRISON WALLS

I broke that promise to my mom when I covered a performance by legendary rock-and-roll singer Chuck Berry at the Missouri State Penitentiary in Jefferson City. I was surprised that my news director would give me the assignment. I was a twenty-three-year-old female reporter going into an all-male prison, and I was going solo. But I wasn't going to use my gender as an excuse not to cover an assigned story. Speaking with one of the other reporters at the station, I was told the media never mixed with the inmates, so I was confident I would not have any direct contact with the prisoners.

As I laid out my clothes for the next day, I thought long and hard about what I should wear. I wanted to be covered up in a loose-fitting outfit, nothing too tight or revealing. I was mindful there would be thousands of men behind bars, some of whom probably hadn't seen a woman in decades.

A half hour later, I finally settled on a black blazer with a red, neckline blouse and black slacks. I certainly wouldn't slip through unnoticed, but at least I wouldn't attract the wrong kind of attention.

The next morning, as I loaded my news vehicle with my camera, deck, tripod, and light case, I wasn't afraid. I focused on how exciting it was going to be to see Chuck Berry, one of my mom's favorite singers.

When I pulled up to the penitentiary, it was massive and intimidating. I had driven by this prison for years when I was in college, but I had never noticed that it was like a fortress. I drove through the huge iron gates, and as they shut behind me, my heart started pounding. It finally hit me that I was all alone on this shoot, and I was about to go inside a maximum security prison, home to men who had probably committed unspeakable crimes.

I walked in, loaded down with my television gear. I carried my camera and deck on one shoulder and held the tripod in my hand. I could leave the lights behind because it would be an outdoor shoot on the prison grounds with plenty of natural light.

I joined other media personalities who were there to cover the concert—crews from the local NBC and ABC affiliates and a few newspaper and radio folks. All of them were men.

After security cleared us, they gave us a few ground rules: Don't talk to the inmates. Don't cross the yellow tape that separates you from the prisoners. Don't ever, for any reason, stray from the guards who are escorting you.

I had no idea what awaited me inside the prison walls. As the guards led us deeper into the prison, shuffling between two strips of three- or four-inch-wide yellow tape, voices reverberated. I couldn't believe my eyes. There were dozens of inmates lined up alongside the tape. They could actually reach out and touch us. The men were black and white, young and old. Some were huge, like bodybuilders, while others were small, and some looked downright creepy.

To my surprise, they started screaming for me as soon as they saw me.

"Romona, that's Romona Robinson!"

"You're looking good, baby!"

"I watch you every weekend."

"Peace, sister!"

"Power to the people!"

"Black power!"

"Right on, sistah!"

Some of their chants were indications of just how long they had been behind bars.

The men stared at me—now hundreds of them—never taking their eyes off me as I walked by. I saw looks of appreciation, gratitude, and lust. Some of the stares were blank, a few even sinister. Some of the inmates blew kisses, while a few moaned as they called my name. I was uncomfortable, to say the least, but I was careful not to show it.

The guards kept us moving. As I lugged my equipment, the inmates' chants of "We love you, Romona!" started to turn bitter.

"Why is our sistah the only one loaded down with that camera shit?"

"Carry that for her, motherf***s—now!"

"Y'all better help her with that shit!"

Suddenly, the other reporters, even the newspaper and radio guys, grabbed my equipment. The inmates kept hollering, "You better carry that for her. Our sweet Romona shouldn't have to work that hard!"

I knew from the fan mail I received I had a following behind bars, but this experience added another dimension to my popularity entirely.

I obeyed the rules and did not speak to any of the inmates, but they wouldn't stop talking to me. A few reached over the yellow tape to shake my hand. We paused as our news caravan waited for an escort outside, and some inmates began calling out their stories. One said that he wished he had stayed in school and out of trouble so he could date a girl like me. Another talked about not listening to his mom, and I remember another saying he had gotten involved with the wrong crowd. The guard shot me a look to see whether I was afraid.

Surprisingly, my fear had dissipated. I knew they were criminals, but so many of them looked as if they could be my uncle, my brother, or my cousin. The more I looked at them, the more I wanted to know. How could some of these men be locked up when they had smiles that could light up a room? Of course, I wasn't allowed to ask. One prisoner shouted at me, asking if I had a boyfriend. I just smiled, but suddenly he pushed through the crowd, jumped beneath the tape, and grabbed me in a big bear hug as another inmate quickly snapped a picture. In that moment, I was frozen with fear, but somehow I produced a rigid smile. Frankly, I was shocked they had a camera. The guard, sensing this could easily get out of control, yelled for the inmates to get back behind the tape and motioned for me to walk shoulder to shoulder between him and another guard. We could hear Chuck Berry and his band warming up outside.

Finally, all of the inmates were led outside to a roped-off area. The media were escorted onto the grounds as the band began to play. Chuck Berry sounded great, but he looked much smaller in person than he did on television. His skin was oily, no doubt from the extreme heat of the day. He opened with one of his hits, which had the inmates in a frenzy. I couldn't wait to get closer to get pictures of him and his famous guitar.

As we approached the stage, something happened that I could never have anticipated. The inmates started chanting, "Romona! Romona! Romona!" so loudly that they drowned out the music. I didn't know whether to ignore them or acknowledge them. So, I did what came naturally: I waved.

Wrong move! The place erupted into a roar. "Romona! Romona! Romona!" they chanted more loudly. All of a sudden, Chuck Berry waved his hands, signaling the band to stop playing. "Who are you?" he said into the microphone, looking straight at me.

Standing about twenty feet from the stage, I paused for a second and then nervously shouted, "Romona Robinson with Channel 13, sir."

"I want you out now!"

"With all due respect, Mr. Berry, I'm here to cover your concert. Why am I being asked to leave?" I shouted firmly, making sure he could hear me.

"I want you out!" he shouted again. By this time, the inmates had grown upset. Some chanted, "No! Don't make her leave!" while others yelled, "Romona, don't go!"

I was defiant, knowing I had as much right as anyone to cover this concert, and my station would be terribly upset if I didn't get the story. Finally, two guards standing next to me said, "Romona, please just leave. This could turn into a riot." I looked around, and I saw that the inmates had indeed become agitated. So, I grabbed my equipment and left.

The incident left me with a lot of unanswered questions. For days, all I could think about were the inmates I had seen, mostly black men. Some of them were handsome. They looked like they could have been anything in the world had they not chosen a life of crime. Why had God sent me there? What was the takeaway? Was I supposed to tell their story?

All questions I didn't yet have answers to.

Chapter 23

TIME FOR CHANGE

Working in Jefferson City was an incredible learning experience. After a year, I was comfortable in my weekend anchor role. I covered several big stories, and I became a pretty good writer and producer. I finally learned how to shoot video, and I even did some fill-in sports anchoring.

As much fun as I was having, though, I was still the weekend anchor in a small television market. It was time for me to move on to a larger market and take another step toward my goal of becoming the primary anchor of a weeknight newscast in a major city.

I put together what I thought was an impressive résumé tape. In television, it's what we call a short, attention-grabbing videotape that showcases your best work. You only have a few minutes—or sometimes seconds—to get the news director hooked since they receive hundreds, if not thousands, of audition tapes.

I was told that news directors liked to see versatility and depth. I included my coverage of President Reagan, exclusive interviews with Governor Kit Bond, a few breaking news stories, and of course, the bear story, which was certainly memorable if nothing else. I put a clip of my anchoring last on the tape, even though it was the position I wanted.

I felt it was important to show I was a hardworking street reporter, not just a pretty, young face sitting at a desk. My philosophy was that if I demonstrated my writing and reporting skills, I would be a stronger, more well-rounded candidate, one who didn't mind getting her hands dirty. I learned that from watching Walter Cronkite. He anchored the news, but during the big stories, he went into the field to report. I remember thinking he could do it all.

Months later, in August 1985, I accepted an anchor/ reporter job at WCIV-TV in Charleston, South Carolina. Somewhat uneasily, Charleston took me far from my home state and my family. It was a big move. Missouri was all I'd ever known. As I learned in Genesis 12:1, Abram stepped out on faith when the Lord told him to "go from your country, your people, and your father's household to the land that I will show you." I wasn't sure whether God was telling me to give up my security blanket, but my desire to succeed was my driving motivation.

Charleston was a beautiful, old city, rich in tradition and Southern culture. When I arrived, I was fortunate to snag a very knowledgeable cab driver. I asked him to give me a quick tour of the city before I arrived at my apartment. The articles and history books I had read didn't capture the essence of this southern city. It was spectacular, like a step back in time. There were people in horse-drawn carriages, and hotel bellmen were dressed in historic garb, wearing huge top hats and old-fashioned suits. We drove along the southern tip of the peninsula overlooking the waterfront, an area called "The Battery," which was lined with exquisite waterfront homes possessing old-world charm.

"This is the first time I've ever seen palm trees in person," I told the driver.

He quickly corrected me. "Palmettos. They're generally smaller than palms."

When the driver dropped me off at my apartment, I thanked him for the wealth of information.

* * * *

Getting acclimated to how things were done at Channel 4 wasn't difficult. I immediately struck a rapport with the photographers. I had a great time producing stories with one photographer in particular named Keith. He shot beautiful, creative video for all of the stories he covered, whether it was breaking news or the county fair, and he came to work excited every day. His energy and enthusiasm for his craft were contagious, and I fed off of it.

However, I guess Keith and I were having too much fun. One day, we were split up by one of the news managers. It was no secret that she did not like me. For months I had tried to win her over. A male colleague said, "Face it, Romona. When she looks at you, she sees a tall, attractive woman with a great personality that lights up a room." It was a strange form of flattery, but to my mind, it didn't excuse her unprofessional behavior.

This manager clearly had it in for me. Several months later, she was the one who sent me on the assignment that landed me face-to-face with the Grand Dragon of the Ku

Klux Klan. That same colleague had confided to me that my manager didn't care for blacks. She gave me the story hoping I would refuse it, giving her grounds to force me out. When I returned to the station after my coverage, the news manager was waiting for me. "How was it, Romona?" she yelled from a few yards away.

I smiled, desperately trying to keep my professional cool. "It was really interesting to hear a man spew so much hatred so openly. I kind of felt sorry for him. It must take so much energy to walk around hating other people for no reason. But I've got to give it to the Klan. At least you know exactly how they feel about you. They don't pretend to be unprejudiced," I said matter-of-factly.

"By the way, Romona," she said with a smirk. "I don't need the sound you got. I would never use an interview with the Klan on air."

Maybe my news manager thought she could scare me, but what she didn't know was that I lived by faith, not fear. Instead of bringing me down, she was making me stronger. No way was I going to hightail it out of there at the first sign of trouble. No one could use the N-word and hurt me. *I am a child of God, protected from evil and evildoers*, I thought.

The Grand Dragon, his head covered or uncovered, was no threat to me. The word "nigger" didn't apply to me. My mom had taught me so. She told us it was an ugly word white people had made up to describe us during slavery. It could only hurt us if that's what we thought of ourselves.

Chapter 24

HURRICANE CHARLIE

One day, we heard the sound of rocks pelting the roof of the TV station. Looking out as the wind whipped debris against the windows, we saw swift and heavy rain. We had been preparing for a tropical storm. Our meteorologist had warned of an impending hurricane, but it was impending no more. It was August 1986, and Hurricane Charlie had arrived.

Our producer yelled for me and a photographer named Florian. "It's golf-ball-sized hail you hear! They're calling for the hurricane to come ashore. Trees and power lines are down. There are a few buildings reportedly damaged. I need the two of you to get out and cover it." Growing up in Missouri, I had only seen pictures of hurricanes on television. Actually covering one as a news story riddled my body with anxiety.

It was only expected to be a "minor" hurricane by the time it reached Charleston, which meant the maximum sustained winds would be about seventy-five miles an hour. I knew this would be a huge story for me, but at what cost?

We drove down to Folly Beach to see how high the waves had gotten and to look for any damage or destruction. In the car, we felt the wind's intensity. The vehicle swayed from side to side as Florian kept a tight grip on the steering wheel. The hurricane tossed leaves and tree limbs into our path, and some smacked against our windshield. We passed downed power lines and violently swaying trees. The wind ripped siding off of homes. We heard from the station that residents were boarding up their houses, and some might start evacuating because of flooding.

When we arrived at Folly Beach, we pulled around to the rear of one of the hotels and looked out at the ocean. "Oh my God!" I blurted out.

I had never seen anything like it. The waves were about twenty feet high, bursting out of the ocean and smacking against the breakwall of the hotel. Florian pulled his windbreaker over his head and sprinted from the car to get pictures. I ran right behind him.

The winds were strong and intense. As I stood in front of the camera to do my stand-up along the breakwater, a giant wave crashed over the wall and smacked me right on the head. It tossed me a few feet and knocked me to the ground. To my surprise, I scrambled back up—completely drenched—and continued reporting. Florian couldn't help but laugh, telling me I looked like a drowned rat.

We had a good chuckle and headed back to the station to dry off. I was proud of my toughness that day. The dangerous and exciting coverage of a hurricane wasn't half bad for a girl who had grown up crying every time the wind blew.

Chapter 25

A Lesson on Slavery

My time in Charleston was a tremendous learning experience. I got chances to do great, teachable stories, and what's more, I had come through them stronger than ever. One story in particular remains etched in my memory: the Old Slave Mart Museum. In doing my research, I learned that Charleston's exquisite façade had a dark side; its riches had been paid for, in part, by slavery.

I had no idea that the Old Slave Mart Museum even existed. As my photographer and I arrived, I marveled at how ancient it looked. It sat on a quaint cobblestone street in Charleston called Chalmers. The façade of the building had high, octagonal pillars and a large iron gate. I was told the building had been painstakingly preserved. Inside, I was greeted by the curator, whom I would interview.

As the curator spoke, I forced eye contact with her. The museum was overpowering; it stole my attention as soon as I walked in. She explained that the slave mart was the actual building where slave auctions were held in Charleston. In one large room, slaves stood on auction tables so slave owners could inspect them. After the Civil War, the building was turned into a museum.

As we talked, I looked around in disbelief. I was unprepared for what I saw. On the floor sat replicas of slaves with chains and shackles around their necks and ankles, their clothing stuffed with straw to make them look more human. I don't remember details of their faces, but I know their heads were fashioned from straw and fabric, and they had black buttons for eyes. I was horrified, but I managed to mask my emotions, remembering I was on assignment, until she showed me what looked like an ancient scroll. I don't remember whether it was authentic or a copy, but she removed it from a case, warning that it had to be handled with extreme care. It listed the slaves who were sold at the slave mart. It contained mostly first names along with gender: *Bob, a strong male. Mary, a young female.* It also included the names of the slave owners who purchased them.

My heart sank. The barbarism became all too real. I was overcome with sorrow. I had no way of knowing whether any of the slaves were my ancestors, but I was visibly shaken. I was torn between appreciation that the museum had been preserved and the pain of a national past that was too much to bear.

My mind raced. To think, this was once legal in this country, that the children born to slaves faced the same bleak future as their parents. They couldn't marry or learn to read or write. Could I ever have dreamed of becoming a journalist had it not been for my ancestors' sacrifice?

The Civil War, the Emancipation Proclamation, the Thirteenth Amendment, and Dr. King were all key forces that catalyzed change in our country. Today, African-Americans like me can enjoy freedom and equality because of the horrors our ancestors endured.

Chapter 26

A GOOD MAN IS GOOD ENOUGH

Enjoying Charleston's nightlife, I harkened back to memories of my college days when girls hoping to someday marry talked about "the list." You know the one, where young women listed the must-haves of their perfect mate:

1. Must have a college degree

2. Must have a job

3. Must own a home or have his own apartment

4. Must have his own car—preferably a luxury model

5. Must be tall, dark, and handsome (in fact, this might be number one)

6. Must have no baggage—having children is a no-no

On the rare days I wasn't completely exhausted from my weekend anchoring, producing, and reporting duties, I hung out on Saturday nights with a few of the single people I had met in the business. My college sweetheart, Carl, lived in Washington, D.C. He and I managed to keep our long-distance romance intact, visiting each other once a month.

I vividly recall one night out on the town with a female reporter at a rival station who asked if I wanted to get a drink after work. She was a striking young black woman with flawless, chocolate skin and beautiful, cropped hair. She had an awesome figure, and her walk screamed confidence. Like me, she was eager to climb the business ladder. However, that was about all we had in common, I soon found out.

The two of us walked into the club together. It felt like all eyes immediately focused on us. The music was blaring, and the psychedelic lights were swirling across the dance floor, producing just enough light in the dark room to find seats. I recall there were men aplenty. I smiled as we walked by a few handsome onlookers, though not forgetting I was spoken for.

We took a seat and ordered drinks. We bobbed our heads to the music and spoke at the top of our lungs in order to be heard. I noticed three men across the bar were checking us out, and one in particular had eyes for my friend.

"Someone is checking you out, girl!" I yelled to her over the loud music, but he had already started walking toward our table. I was smiling, but I noticed she wasn't. In fact, she looked tense, like something was wrong. *Does she know this man?* I wondered. *Is he an old boyfriend?* I couldn't ask since her suitor was only a few feet away.

His buddies egged him on, I could tell, though they were trying not to be obvious about it. Standing in front of my girlfriend, appearing confident, the man said, "Hello!"

I've never forgotten what happened next. Smiling, he extended his hand to shake hers, and to my disbelief, she didn't open her mouth to say hello or offer her hand in return. Instead, she folded her arms across her chest, giving him a menacing look. He introduced himself, telling my friend he watched her every night and enjoyed her reporting. But she was still giving him the evil eye, refusing to utter a word. It was as if the smoke-filled room had somehow clouded her good judgment and rendered her unconscious. *Why else would her body language suddenly go stone cold?* I thought.

He positioned his body closer to hers, possibly assuming she couldn't hear him over the deafening music, but even a lip reader could make out "hello" or an extended hand.

I became so uncomfortable and did the only thing I could think of. I quickly stretched out my hand. "Hi, I'm Romona. I guess you don't watch me since you watch that other station," I joked.

"Yes, Romona, I've checked out your channel, too," he said, smiling and looking a little more at ease.

"Thank you," I said, laying on the charm a little too thick. I tried to be as warm and personable as I could, hopefully making up for my girlfriend's stoic behavior. She breathed heavily as if she couldn't wait for him to leave.

"Well, it was nice meeting the two of you," he said softly, trying not to show any sign that his feelings were hurt.

"Thank you, and thanks again for watching us," I replied with another handshake and a smile.

He slowly walked back to his friends. They were laughing now, almost falling off their barstools, knowing he had struck out.

"What's wrong?" I asked loudly, getting within inches of her ear to be sure she could hear me. "Do you know him? Why were you so cold?"

Her response went against everything I had ever been taught. "Yes, I know him," she said, her arms still folded and her body still stiff. "He works as a manager at the McDonald's around the corner from where I live. I go in there to get my morning coffee."

"And what did he do to you?" I shouted.

"Nothing," she yelled back. "He just works at McDonald's, and I don't have to be nice to any low-wage worker just because they watch me on television. He probably doesn't have a college degree, he's average-looking, and he probably lives with his mother."

My eyebrows lowered. I frowned and pasted my lips together in confusion. "He just wanted to say hello, and you made him feel so low. I could see it in his eyes," I snapped. I couldn't hide my disgust.

"I don't care. He's nothing, and he's a nobody. He doesn't check off any of my boxes for a mate. I mean, what future does he have managing a McDonald's?" she fired back.

"It's not like he asked you to marry him. He was just being nice!" I was so steamed at her, afraid that the man had associated me with her ugliness.

Our fun night out was over, and it would be our last. I knew I could never be friends with someone who treated others with such disrespect. As I headed home, I thought of my mom and how I had been raised. She always said,

"Never forget who you are and where you came from. Don't let anyone change who you are."

Don't worry, Mom, I thought. *I never will.*

Chapter 27

SHOULD I STAY OR SHOULD I GO?

I felt a transformation taking place. All of my hard work as a reporter and anchor was paying off. I saw big improvements in my work, my speech, and my delivery. I was different emotionally as well; my compassion for people had grown deeper. As a reporter and as a human being, I cared about what people were going through and their life struggles, no matter their job title or where they came from.

It was February 1987. I had been in Charleston for a year and a half, and I liked the town, in spite of its ghosts from the past. My news manager called me into his office. I was nervous, wondering whether I had done something wrong. My anxiety quickly turned to happiness when he told me the station wanted to offer me a long-term contract to anchor on weekends and report on weeknights. He complimented my work and my hustle in the field. He talked about how my live reporting had improved.

"If I sign a new deal, would I be considered for the main anchor job on weeknights should it become available?" I asked, thinking about my potential future at Channel 4.

Leaning back in his chair, the warmth in his face suddenly dissipated. "The position isn't available. We expect our main anchor to be here for some time," he said firmly.

"I know it's not available now. I'm just asking hypothetically. If it were available in the future, would I be given the opportunity or at least be considered?"

He evaded the question again. "I don't make promises," he said, agitated that I was pressing the issue.

"I understand you can't make promises, but I was hoping for some assurance that I would be considered for the main anchor job if I sign a long-term deal. You just said how much I've grown, and I'll continue to work hard and learn."

"We're not talking about the future right now. I want you to continue anchoring the weekend newscast, Romona," he said definitively. Of course, I knew that his hedging meant I'd probably never get a shot at weeknights.

I recalled a conversation I'd had with someone in management about my career aspirations. He confided that yes, there had been a few African-American anchors in the morning and afternoon in Charleston, but never a black primary evening anchor, male or female, in his lifetime. He didn't believe the city was "ready" for a person of color in such a prominent, high-profile position anytime in the near future. I appreciated his candor, although I understood what that meant for my career.

I told my news manager I wanted to weigh my options. I was completely honest with him. I loved my job, I wanted to become a main anchor for the six o'clock and eleven o'clock evening newscasts someday, and I hoped it would be at Channel 4. I talked about my five years of television experience, the latter two with WCIV. I knew I still had a lot to learn, but I wanted the opportunity to advance at the station.

What he said next floored me.

"I don't think you understand. You either sign this new deal, or we're considering other candidates and you're out." He showed no emotion. "I'm not going to let you stay here and look for another job."

I couldn't believe what I was hearing. He had just showered me with compliments about my work. Where had the love gone so quickly?

"Take some time to think about it, and give me your answer in the morning."

That night, I sat alone in my apartment, stared at the walls, and mulled over my short career in Charleston. *Maybe this isn't the station for me,* I thought. *Maybe it's time to move on. Am I willing to stay in Charleston and wait, hoping one day I'll be promoted?*

I wrestled with the decision. I knew this was one of those life-changing moments Mom had told me about. However, she always told us that if we worked hard and were lucky enough to get a good-paying job, try to keep it because jobs are hard to come by. But I was an adult now, and it meant I had to make adult decisions.

I took the news manager's words to bed. The more I tossed and turned, the angrier I became. I had twenty-four hours to decide my future, so I started doing what I always did—I prayed, asking God to give me an answer. I told Him how alone I felt. The weight of my decision was like a boulder on my back. Fear suffocated my thoughts. I didn't want to call my mom or Beulah or anyone else to ask what I should do. If I made the wrong decision, it was going to be mine to make.

How could I stay at a station I knew might never promote me? Fear crept in at the possibility of being out of work, and tears followed. The voice of the devil danced in my head. "Where is your God?" he whispered. "Where is the savior you gave your life to on the banks of the Mississippi? You've spent your life worshipping an imaginary God, you silly girl." Laughter followed.

The devil had taken a space in my head and parked. I rolled over to reach my nightstand. I grabbed my Bible and snuggled into my covers, just as my mom and I had done decades ago. I can't recall the Scripture I read, but the phrases Mom had uttered hundreds of times came back to me: "God will make a way out of no way…He will never leave you nor forsake you." The memory of Mom and Scripture seemed like the voice of God telling me exactly what I needed to do.

Morning came far too soon. When I arrived at work, I was immediately called into my manager's office.

"What's it gonna be, Romona? You gonna take it or leave it?" he asked with an air of confidence.

I looked him in the eye. With no other job prospects, and not knowing how I would pay my bills, I said, "I think I'll leave it."

"Are you certain this is what you want to do?" he asked, surprised.

"You haven't given me much of a choice now, have you?" I said. "I either stay and sign a long-term contract, hoping I might be promoted someday, or I leave, right?"

He gave me a stern look and ordered me to pack my things and leave the building immediately.

Wow! The impact of what I had just done hit me like a freight train. I made the slow walk to my car, toting every piece of my eighteen-month existence at WCIV in a box. My head hung low and my heart was crushed. Tears rolled down my face as I sat in my car before starting the engine. I got it. There were not many blacks in primary anchor roles across the country, so the powers that be in smaller markets were uneasy about having blacks in such high-profile positions. I wish I could say I had taken a stand for all African-Americans who might be denied a promotion based on the color of their skin, but that would be a lie. I made the decision on principle. I had five years of anchoring and reporting experience, and I would not be denied an opportunity to advance my career, especially because of my race.

Chapter 28
OUT OF A JOB

I was out of a job with very little money saved. My quick exit had given me no time to put together a résumé tape, but two photographers at the station put together some of my best work for me. I sent out about fifteen résumés and audition tapes to television markets across the country—a few large-market stations, but mostly medium-sized ones.

My coverage of Hurricane Charlie was a huge hit with news directors. I started getting calls right away. Most didn't have job openings, but they wanted to tell me what a fantastic job I had done covering the storm. Even though I had gotten knocked to the ground by the waves and the wind, I had the presence of mind to get back up and keep reporting.

When weeks and months went by with no job offers, I started to second-guess my decision. *What kind of smart, sane person quits a good-paying job without another waiting in the wings?* I thought.

I asked God, "How could you let me do such a stupid thing? I thought you were supposed to watch over me!" My faith was being tested. Fear wracked my body as I continued to rant to God. "I'm out of work with very little savings, and I'm scared, but you already know that, don't you?"

I talked to Him morning, noon, and night. Some days I bargained with Him. I begged Him. I made promises. I did what I always did when I was afraid—I grabbed my Bible and started reading at whatever page it opened to. I didn't tell my mom I didn't have a job. I knew she would worry and probably tell me to come home, but I had made this career decision, right or wrong, and I had to live with it.

Chapter 29
HIS CHEATIN' HEART

My boyfriend was still living and working in Washington, D.C. He immediately insisted I move in with him before I drained my savings. It was a tough decision. I had never lived with a man, and I had told myself I never would unless we were married. Still, it was either move in with him or go home and admit to Mom I had walked out on a new contract offer.

I settled in Washington and sent out my few remaining audition tapes. A few more weeks went by, and the phone didn't ring. To make ends meet until another television job came along, I applied for a sales job at a department store. They hired me on the spot as a Lancôme makeup consultant.

As the days and weeks went by, I became depressed. Driving home from work, I saw news crews along the highway covering stories, and I longed to be a part of it all again. Each night I prayed, crying out, "Lord, how did things go so wrong? I know it was you who told me not to accept the contract offer. You've known my dream of becoming a primary evening anchor since I was six years old. You were there when I made the declaration and when Momma said I could do it. Is this some sort of test? Have you abandoned me now?"

I grew more and more frustrated because there was no sign God was even listening to me. *Where is this God I've prayed to all of my life?* I wondered. *Has He really deserted me?* I had worshipped God and believed in Him and feared Him, but now, my faith was failing me. I simply had no answers. I was just one sad soul.

* * * *

I believed in the love I felt for my boyfriend. However, living with a man for the first time taught me a lot about trust in a relationship. We were committed to one another, and I believed I was his only love.

One day, while I was making room in his closet for my things, I stumbled upon a box of love letters. I started to read them. "Aww," I sighed with a smile. The letters were from me, some dating back to college when we had been apart during the summer break. I was so touched he had saved them.

But then there were letters from other girls, some of them dating back to college. "I love you. I can't wait till you come home for summer break again," read one letter. Another said, "I'm glad I'm still your one and only."

When Carl came home, I didn't tell him I discovered the letters. It took everything in me to hold back my anger, but at the moment I was more preoccupied with a nagging pain in my abdomen. It had been bothering me for weeks. I hadn't seen a doctor because I was so busy finding a job, but the pain was becoming unbearable.

I remember the shocking results. The gynecologist told me my pap smear was abnormal and that I needed a laparoscopy. Based on other symptoms I was having, he suspected cancer.

It can't be! I thought. *I'm in my twenties. I'm too young to have cancer!*

I knew what I had to do. I didn't have a church home in Washington, so I asked a neighbor to find a minister for me. I needed someone to pray with me. A female pastor came to our apartment, and we prayed together and recited a verse from Psalm 23: "Though I walk through the valley of the shadow of death, I will fear no evil: for thou art with me."

My outpatient procedure was scheduled for a few weeks later. It was minimally invasive, but it required placing a telescopic rod lens connected to a camera into my navel through a small incision. General anesthesia was required for the less than two-hour procedure. After the surgery, the doctor said I would be extremely sore. I would need help getting in and out of bed and bathing myself for a few days.

My mom (whom I did eventually tell I was no longer in television), planned to send my little sister to D.C. to help so Carl wouldn't have to miss work. But Carl wouldn't hear of it, telling my mom he would take time off work to care for me.

On the day of the surgery, he was so loving. He took me to the hospital at 5:30 a.m., and I was out of recovery by 2:00 p.m. The doctor had great news: it was not cancer. It was a benign cyst. I was sent home with a clean bill of health.

I could barely walk, though. The laparoscopy had left me in excruciating pain. I ambled like a zombie, even with

Carl's help. Even though I had just had the procedure, I felt guilty. Carl had stayed with me all morning and afternoon, but it seemed as if he had things to do. I told him if he wanted a break or had errands to run, I'd be all right by myself for a couple of hours.

He left about 5:30 p.m., tucking me tightly in bed. He even phoned his younger sister to come over and keep me company. But when she tired of waiting for Carl to come home later that night, she went to sleep on the couch.

It was 9:00 p.m., then 11:00 p.m., and Carl hadn't returned. He hadn't called, either. I wasn't sure what to think. As I lay in bed, I yelled for his sister to help me get to the bathroom, but she never woke up. The stitches in my belly hurt just calling out to her.

I finally decided to get myself up. I inched toward the end of the bed, grunting in pain. I tried to lift myself onto the edge of the bed, both hands perched underneath my butt. Instead, I fell backward onto the bed. Determined, I pushed myself up again, and again I fell flat on my back. With all the exertion, I suddenly lost control of my bladder.

I lay in the wet bed for hours. I couldn't take it anymore. I was cold, and my clothes and bed linens were soaked. Once again, I moved toward the edge of the bed, but this time, I misjudged the distance and fell onto the floor, busting my stitches. Rubbing my fingers over the wound, I could feel I was bleeding.

I was on the floor for hours. I was cold. I didn't have the strength to pull the covers down over me. As I lay there shivering, I thought about a lot of things. I wondered whether this was what it was like for women who stayed with men who didn't treat them right. Did they stay out of necessity because they were unemployed, or was it the fear of being without a man?

What am I doing here? I wondered at that moment. I was a bright, educated, strong woman. I was with a man who had cheated on me, and now, apparently, had abandoned me when I needed him the most.

I replayed in my mind the day I almost married Carl. Shortly before I moved to D.C., he surprised me by asking me to marry him. It was nothing romantic as I always dreamed a proposal of marriage would be. One evening, after dinner at his apartment, he said spontaneously, "Will you marry me?" I was at a loss for words. Carl was my college sweetheart, but I didn't feel I was ready for marriage. I didn't know what to say, and I was afraid of hurting his feelings, so I said yes.

He wanted to get married quickly, a simple courthouse ceremony. Again, I agreed, although I knew in my heart it wasn't what I wanted. In the days that followed, I was extremely nervous. How could I tell him I had changed my mind?

"What's wrong, honey? You can't sleep?" he asked one night. "You look a hundred miles away. Is something bothering you?"

He gave me an opening. I should have taken it and said, "I don't want to get married!" But I just couldn't.

Finally, time had run out, and our wedding day arrived. It was a late February morning. Carl came in to wake me up and said, "You won't believe what's going on out there." Perplexed, I got up, looking and feeling disheveled because I hadn't slept at all. "It's snowing, and it's coming down hard!"

We turned on the news to find out the city was shut down, including the courthouses. "Thank you, thank you, Lord!" I murmured.

Carl was crushed. "We'll reschedule tomorrow," he said lovingly.

"Sure we will," I replied, knowing I had no intention of doing so. Somehow, I would work up the nerve to tell him I wasn't ready to get married.

Being skittish about marriage wasn't the whole truth. My inner voice told me that this was not the man God had sent for me.

Carl and I had practiced our vows weeks before: "To have and to hold, in sickness and in health." But now, I was lying by myself on the cold floor. How could I marry someone who wasn't there for me in sickness? If I hadn't known before, I knew now. There was no looking back.

At 5:30 a.m., after I had been on the floor for more than six hours, Carl finally returned.

"Romona, what are you doing down there? Are you all right?" he asked with of look great concern.

I was silent, looking up at him as he hovered over me on his knees. "I'm fine," I said, my voice barely audible. "I was trying to get to the bathroom and didn't make it."

"I'm so sorry I wasn't here," he said.

Carl helped me up and made sure I was comfortable. But he never explained where he had been all night.

The next day, I could tell he was wondering why I was being so nice to him. I was good to him because he had always been good to me. But that night on the floor, an alarm had gone off in my head. Carl loved me; he just couldn't love only me. I knew this was not the type of man I could ever build a life with, and he was not a man God would choose for me.

Chapter 30
A NEW BEGINNING

After a few months of pushing Lancôme products, my life took an unexpected turn in August 1987. I went home and checked the messages on my answering machine, as I did every day, thinking, *Will this be the day the Lord answers my prayers?*

And it was! Unbelievably, there were three messages from news directors in Philadelphia, Des Moines, and Cleveland. All of them wanted to fly me out for an interview.

God finally showed up, I thought. *He hasn't abandoned me.* I started crying and praising Him out loud. "Lord, thank you! My faith had failed me, and fear convinced me you'd turned your back on me. How could I have ever doubted you?"

One of those jobs would be mine, I was certain. I booked all three interviews within a whirlwind, thirty-hour period. I wanted to get to all three cities fast so none of the stations would have a chance to cancel.

First, I flew to Philadelphia in the early morning and interviewed at KYW. A few hours later, I rushed to catch a flight to Des Moines, Iowa, only stopping to freshen up in the airport restroom. Later that night, it was off to WUAB in Cleveland, Ohio. I spent the night in Cleveland and interviewed at the station the next morning.

I was most interested in working in Philadelphia because it was the third-largest television market in the country. I knew if I worked hard, I might be able to launch myself into a network job. During the interview, however, the news director talked to me about a weekend anchor position. I had worked weekends since I started in the business, and it was important to me to become the main anchor of a weeknight newscast. I knew I couldn't afford to be choosy, but I believed I had the talent and experience to do it.

I told the Philly news director I would consider the offer and get back to him with my answer. Then I dashed to the airport and flew to Des Moines. Iowa was never on my list of places I wanted to work. It was far from my family, and I didn't know anyone who lived there. Still, I figured I should go to the interview just in case Philly or Cleveland didn't pan out. What was most important was getting back into the business. If it meant taking a job somewhere I wasn't crazy about, I was prepared to do it.

The news director in Des Moines was nice, and so were the people I met in the newsroom. I remember smiling, trying to pretend I was interested in the job. Then the news director threw a wrench in my plans by asking whether I could spend the afternoon there to meet the general manager and the evening reporters and anchors. I had to come up with a good excuse because I could not and would not miss my flight to Cleveland. I was quick to answer that I was in the middle of a move and had to be out of my apartment the next day. It was sort of true. He said he understood and would be in touch.

I managed to get out of Des Moines on time and arrived in Cleveland later that evening. I didn't sleep at all, checking out every local newscast. I wanted to see what Clevelanders were accustomed to watching. All night in my hotel room, I wondered, *Is this it? A new beginning?*

The next morning, a cab took me to Parma, Ohio, a suburb about twenty miles outside of Cleveland. I walked into an unfinished, vacant newsroom, where the news director, Dan Acklen, and his assistant were waiting for me. Dan was a tall, stocky man who looked like a former wrestler or linebacker. But he was soft-spoken, and there was a gentle simplicity about him. We talked for a few hours, and he gave me a brief history of Cleveland, its people, its diversity, and its problems and successes.

I was frightened and a little skeptical when Dan explained the tensions between Cleveland television stations and the NAACP. The civil rights organization was threatening to boycott Cleveland television stations because they did not have enough minority representation. I couldn't believe that in 1987, Clevelanders had never seen a black woman anchor a prime-time evening newscast. He told me if I were offered the job, I would make history as the city's first black female evening anchor, but he was quick to explain it wasn't the reason he was considering me for the job. He raved about my audition tape, calling my reporting impressive and describing my anchoring as warm and friendly, yet credible and authoritative.

Later that day, I accepted the position of primary anchor for Channel 43's brand-new ten o'clock evening newscast.

Thank you, Lord!

Chapter 31

SHOWTIME

Little did I know that being the first black woman on Cleveland's evening news would incite hatred.

Dan had assembled a great group of anchors and reporters and an entire staff in a few short months. When the ten o'clock news debuted in January 1988, it was a special night for all of us, but there was also a great deal of pressure. Many articles had been written about the upcoming ten o'clock news. Some wondered whether it would survive in a traditional eleven o'clock news market.

Not surprisingly, there was a lot of attention on Cleveland's first black female weeknight anchor. I heard the word "first" a lot. On one hand, I was proud. On the other hand, I felt as if I carried the weight of the black community on my shoulders. *Will I be good enough? Will I fit in? How will I be perceived?* I wondered. After all, I was an outsider. At least, that's how I saw myself.

Deep down, I didn't care about the naysayers. I had achieved my goal. I was a main anchor in the ninth-largest TV market in the country. What did concern me, though, was the hate mail I started receiving about a month before I went on the air from people claiming to be members of the Ku Klux Klan in Akron, Ohio.

The first one read, "Eddie Murphy is not a black man. Eddie Murphy is not a Negro. Eddie Murphy is a monkey. What does that make you?"

Another writer had taped a picture of former Miss America Vanessa Williams to the letter. The caption under her name read, "This is not Vanessa Williams." Below, there was a picture of an ape with a caption that read, "This is Vanessa Williams...and so are you."

A third letter read, "We don't need a nigger anchor in Cleveland. We have beautiful white anchors. Go back where you came from."

I tried to ignore the letters. I had a television debut to look forward to in just a few weeks.

* * * *

It was finally January 1988, and I felt as if all of Northeast Ohio was watching as the ten o'clock news debuted. I stepped into our newly built studios and walked past millions of dollars of equipment and new furniture, a crew chomping at the bit to do a real show after weeks of rehearsing, and lights so bright they were almost blinding. There were four cameras, all pointing at the anchor desk.

Suddenly, I felt the pressure. My co-anchor, Bob Hetherington, looked ready and confident. But something wasn't quite right with me. Instead of being exuberant about my opening night—the night I had been waiting for all my life—I couldn't stop thinking about those letters I received.

The floor director started to count down. "Ten seconds to air!"

But I wasn't concentrating. I wasn't looking at the words on the teleprompter. Instead, I was picturing viewers at home with white sheets covering their heads, and they were all laughing at me.

"Three, two, one, and you're on!"

I had to perform, and I had to give it my best.

An hour later, I had my first show as an evening news anchor under my belt.

I went on the air for several nights, still trying to ignore the letters, but they ripped at my heart. I only shared the hate mail with my news director. Each time, I would sit in his office and cry. He kept a box of tissues on his desk, and I used many of them. "Why do they hate me?" I asked Dan. "What kind of city is this? What did I do to deserve this?"

His words that day will stick with me for the rest of my life. He said that as a white man, he was embarrassed by the actions of some people of his own race, and he assured me that not every white person in the Cleveland area felt like those idiots. He told me I could turn and run if I wanted, but unfortunately—no matter where I went in this country—I might encounter racism.

I knew he was right. After all, I was probably one of the few blacks who had stared down the Ku Klux Klan in South Carolina and lived to tell about it. But it didn't make the sting of those hurtful words disappear.

What did make them vanish eventually? The wonderful people I worked with and the outpouring of support I received from the people of Northeast Ohio.

* * * *

When I wasn't anchoring the news, I canvassed the region, making four or five appearances a week and talking to any group that would have me. I scoured the east side and west side suburbs and rural areas, too. I was invited to schools and churches, and a fourteen-year-old with a crush invited me to his bar mitzvah. I did the polka at a Polish hall in Parma, and I learned to do the Irish jig (not well) in North Olmsted. Through my community service, I realized those letters had come from a very small group of people who didn't matter to me anymore. I would not waste one more minute of my life thinking about them.

A year passed, and I began to see that Dan was right. Cleveland was home to many first-class people who were hardworking, nurturing, and friendly. During my time at Channel 43, I learned so much, not just about the business but also about the history of the people of Cleveland. It was a blue-collar steel town, and people didn't care whether you were born there as long as you embraced the city and tried to help make a difference.

One of the things I didn't like about Cleveland, though, was how children were portrayed in the media. It seemed as if every station every day ran stories about kids in trouble—kids on drugs, kids in court, truant kids. All negative, especially when it came to the Cleveland school system. Yet, when I visited area schools, I met kids who were chess champions, community volunteers, budding leaders, and young scholars.

One day it hit me: I wanted Northeast Ohio to meet these dynamic kids. I wanted to do a segment that would highlight the positive things kids were doing to improve their lives or the lives of others. Several people told me stories about good kids doing positive things would never fly in Cleveland. I worked in a business where producers love the mantra "If it bleeds, it leads." But I wouldn't be deterred. I was determined to prove them wrong.

Decades later, my segment, called "Romona's Kids," would become an institution in Cleveland, and it is still running today. It is one of my proudest accomplishments. Each week, I highlight the work of a special child who is making a difference in the community. Some are whiz kids, others are inventors. Some make quilts or stuffed animals for sick children, and others volunteer at nursing homes or feed the hungry. I found the list of good kids out there is endless. Through these segments, I've had the privilege to know and work with thousands of teenagers, and I've been able to reach children some said couldn't be reached.

Many of them have powerful stories to tell. Some have made mistakes in their lives but have turned themselves around. Some of my kids have had drinking or drug problems, while others have lived in at-risk or group homes. I found you couldn't exclude these kids. They deserved a chance to change.

I also shared with them my own stories of struggle and how I had overcome obstacles. They enjoyed listening to me, hanging on my every word. I'd remind them that we've all made a wrong turn or two, including me. As teens and young people, sometimes we just do "dumb" things, even when we know we're putting ourselves in danger. We often don't think about dying. We think we're invincible. Even me.

One such lapse in judgment came for me when I was a sophomore in college. I was hanging out with my girlfriend, Cynthia. She was really more like an acquaintance. She had an older brother, Greg, whom I didn't know very well because he didn't attend college with us. It was a Saturday night, and Cynthia asked if I wanted to go along with her and Greg for a fun night out. She said he loved to play a game that entailed jumping over railroad tracks in a car. It sounded somewhat elementary to me, but what the heck—I had nothing else to do. Cynthia raved it had the rush and thrill of an amusement park ride. I had only been on a merry-go-round at our small carnivals at home, so it sounded like fun.

Greg was laying on the horn outside. Our dorm mother, who was seated in the lobby, asked us what the rush was as we ran out to his truck.

Cynthia and I climbed into the back seat of his Jeep, dangling our feet a few inches off the floor, trying not to step on his beer and liquor. Just one glimpse of his bloodshot eyes, and I could tell he had already started to partake.

"Good to see you again, Romona. Are you ever going to go out with me?" he asked.

"The answer is still no, Greg," I responded coyly.

"What's up with that, girl? Do you know how many girls on this campus want me?" he said boastfully.

"No, I didn't know you were so popular. It's not what Cynthia tells me," I said as Cynthia and I giggled.

"Well, I'm glad you decided to come out with me and have some fun. Y'all want a drink?"

"Sure," Cynthia said, grabbing one of the bags and pulling something out called Mad Dog. Cynthia turned the bottle up, guzzled some down, and then handed it off to me. I let 'er rip, too, taking a big gulp. Even though I rarely drank, I did it as to not seem stuffy or that I didn't know how to have a good time.

"I'm gonna take you guys to my favorite place, the train tracks," Greg yelled back at us, laughing.

"Why do you like the tracks?" I asked loudly so he could hear me over the music blasting on the radio.

"It's the most thrilling stunt I do. Wait and see and feel the rush you get."

Greg stretched his arm across the front passenger seat floor and came up with another beer. "Hold on, guys. This is going to be the ride of your lives."

Cynthia held my hand, smiling nervously. We were both a little scared. The Jeep bounced up and down as Greg rolled up on the tracks. Our heads and entire bodies bobbed up and down along with it, sometimes violently, as Greg zigzagged across the tracks, forcing the Jeep to jerk from side to side.

"How do you play this game, Greg? I'm getting dizzy from all of this bouncing!" I yelled.

"Be patient," he snapped. "I stay on the tracks until I see the train."

"Then what?" I asked, leaning closer so he could hear me.

"I wait and wait until the very last second, when it gets real close, and then I jump off the tracks."

"You better jump off before seconds, Greg," I said in a panicked and deliberate voice.

"Girl, I'm not gonna kill us. We're just having fun!"

"Don't worry, Romona. Greg isn't gonna kill us. He knows Mom and Dad would whip his ass if anything happened to me," Cynthia said as we continued to slug the bottle of Mad Dog.

I could feel the sensation of the train before I spotted it.

Greg rolled down his driver's side window. "You guys feel that?" he shouted. The Jeep was vibrating, and I heard faint sounds of metal scraping together. We could see a tiny speck of light in the distance. The train was coming!

Greg pumped up the music even louder, still crisscrossing the tracks, moving toward the sound of the train.

"Here it comes!" he yelled. "It's coming! Do y'all see it?"

Cynthia and I pressed up against the front seats to get a view of the train.

"Oh my God!" I screamed. "It's close! Get off the tracks! Greg, get off the tracks!"

"Not yet, Romona. It's still too far away. It's gotta get closer."

Cynthia joined my pleas, and we yelled at Greg in unison. "Greg, jump off the tracks! You're gonna kill us!"

"No!" he said, laughing. "You two are wusses! We have to wait till the last second. That's the thrill."

"Oh my God!" I shouted, grabbing Cynthia's arm and pressing my body close to hers. The train's lights were blinding us as the conductor lay on his horn.

Blood rushed to my head. Everything was spinning. I wasn't sure if it was the Mad Dog or the mad driver! The train bore down on us. I can't remember how close it was because I closed my eyes and was screaming for dear life.

Between the blaring music and the sound of the train's horn, I could feel we were on a crash course for disaster. Finally—suddenly—with what seemed like seconds to spare, I felt Greg turn the steering wheel, hit the gas, and jump off the tracks.

"Damn that was close!" he screamed with a piercing cry of excitement.

I was speechless for a moment. Cynthia and I were disheveled, and we wiped away tears.

I asked myself later why an otherwise intelligent girl would do something so dumb. *Why was I there, in a vehicle with a driver I knew was intoxicated, playing Russian roulette with his life and mine? Did I think I was invincible?*

I didn't have answers for those questions then. I know now it was only by the grace of God I was not hit and killed by a freight train that night. He was still using me, growing my faith.

Importantly, I learned from that experience, and I never did anything again that went against my best judgment. Like I tell my Romona's Kids, what is most important is learning from the rough road you've traveled and the mistakes you've made. We work hard to change our situation and make better decisions in the future.

Chapter 32
NELSON MANDELA

My skill set continued to grow at Channel 43, not only as an anchor, but as a reporter as well. I was getting opportunities to do great stories.

One of my biggest and most awe-inspiring assignments came in 1990. I was traveling to Detroit to report on a historic visit by South African freedom fighter Nelson Mandela. This was his first visit to the United States since he had been freed from a South African jail earlier that year. Imprisoned for twenty-seven years because of his fight against Apartheid, his story and sacrifice captivated the world.

I was especially intrigued by the issues of faith and fear that Mr. Mandela must have wrestled with during his long years in captivity. Did he fear he'd never go free? Did his faith get him through his darkest days?

My mind drifted back to Martin Luther King Jr. As a child, sitting next to my mom, watching Walter Cronkite talk about Dr. King, I always wished I could meet him because of his courageous fight for equality. Mr. Mandela was a man dedicated to a similar fight against racial oppression.

I remember the morning I was to leave for Detroit to cover Mr. Mandela's visit. The Cleveland skies were bright and blue, and the warmth of the sun made it feel like a perfect

June day. I remember thinking God must have made this a gorgeous day for such a courageous man.

When I arrived in Detroit, I was moved by the throngs of people who had gathered to witness this historic event. Thousands lined the streets and boulevards hoping to get a glimpse of this courageous freedom fighter. I don't think I'd ever witnessed such an enormous crowd. Everyone looked on with anticipation, hope, and enthusiasm. They wore Mandela T-shirts and souvenir buttons and held banners, waving their hands high in the air, hoping when his caravan came through, he would know they cared.

The noise inside the venue was deafening, but suddenly, when the moment was upon us and Mr. Mandela was introduced, you could hear a pin drop. Then the place erupted in cheers as he took the stage. Even though I was trying to remain professional—I was there to get a story, after all—I cheered him on, too. I must admit, my objectivity went out the window the moment I saw him. Here was a man who had given up his freedom to help right a wrong. For me, there was no other side to the story.

Mr. Mandela looked just as he did in his pictures: a slender, dark-skinned man with graying hair and a South African accent that warmed your heart immediately. He was soft-spoken yet authoritative. He had a smile that lit up the room.

Mr. Mandela talked about Apartheid and the oppression that still existed in South Africa. I remember him telling the Detroit crowd that Motown music had inspired him during his quarter of a century in prison.

Many of the people in the crowd were hungry for a hero, and they saw Mandela's visit as a beacon of hope for African-Americans. Some also saw his visit as a concrete opportunity to demand freedom for South African blacks.

Chapter 33
LITTLE RED CORVETTE

After years of hard work, I finally reaped some of the fruits of my labor. My job as an anchor paid enough that I could finally afford to buy a new car. I had driven my old Ford Mustang for years, and it was on its last legs. I knew exactly which car I was going to buy.

The salesman immediately tried to impress me with its sleek, aerodynamic exterior, seventeen-inch alloy wheels, the V-8, 300-horsepower engine, and supple leather seats, but I was already hooked and didn't need a pitch.

"I will take a red one, like the one on the showroom floor," I said to the Chevrolet dealer. "I want a bright, shiny, red Corvette with the drop top."

When I slid into it for a test drive, like a fast-moving storm, my mind drifted back to that day in the soybean fields when I was ten years old, telling my sister, Evonne, "One day, the Lord is going to bless me with a red Corvette, and I'm gonna put the top down and come pick you up, and we'll go for a ride around town just like them."

I bought the car on the spot, and I immediately made plans to drive home to Missouri.

It took me ten hours to make the trip from Cleveland, stopping only twice to gas up. I was so excited I couldn't stop driving.

The weather was perfect as I arrived at Evonne's house in Charleston, Missouri, near where we had grown up. The sun beamed down on my shiny new sports car, just as it had all those years ago in the soybean fields. When I pulled up to the house, I didn't get out of the car; I just honked the horn. Evonne came to the door, unsure at first if the woman behind the large, black shades was me. Then she caught a look at the car with the top down, and she rushed toward it.

"Oh my God, Romona, oh my God! You did it! You did it!"

Just as she was about to jump in the car, she turned around and said, "Oh no, wait!" She ran back inside. A minute later, she sprinted back to the car with her sunglasses on, flashing the biggest grin I'd ever seen. We took off and drove around town with our hair blowing in the wind. We laughed and reminisced, remembering how we had ridden on the back of the old pickup and dreamed of this day. Evonne's eyes began to water, and so did mine. I was emotional because she was. She was always so strong, I don't think I had ever seen her cry. But I always knew this day would come, even when the boys told me it never would.

Chapter 34
UNLUCKY IN LOVE

My career was cruising along now, but in my personal life, I was unlucky in love. On my very first date in Cleveland, I met a gentleman for dinner. I decided to meet him at the restaurant, being cautious because I didn't know him. He was an attractive man with a warm smile that immediately put me at ease.

The date got off to a shaky start, though. Just before dinner, he gave me a beautiful gold bracelet. I thanked him but told him I couldn't accept it; it was too much for a first date. Over dinner, he told me God had brought us together, telling him I was "the one."

Well, God must have forgotten to tell me. I sat there listening intently, but the whole time I was thinking, *How can I get out of this date?*

As soon as we finished dinner, I told him I had had a nice time, but I wasn't looking for a relationship. Leaving the restaurant, he went east, and I went the opposite direction home. *That's the end of that story*, I thought.

I was at home in bed that night, tossing and turning. It was after 3:00 a.m. I thought I was having a nightmare. In my dream, I heard a sawing sound. It was as if someone was quite literally sawing logs. Suddenly, I opened my eyes and realized it wasn't a dream. The noise was coming from downstairs.

I grabbed the phone on my nightstand and jumped to the floor, hiding next to the side of the bed as I called 911. I was so afraid I could barely speak to the dispatcher, who was asking what my emergency was. Then, to my surprise, she said my name.

"Romona? Is this Romona Robinson? Is something wrong?"

"Yes," I said, whispering in the dark. "I think someone's trying to break into my house."

She asked whether I could jump out the window, but I told her no. I was two stories up. "Get into the nearest closet, and don't come out until police arrive," she advised. "There's a squad car in the area, and the police will be there in two minutes."

I crouched in the closet, shivering with fear. My mind was racing. *Who could be trying to break into my home?*

My thoughts were interrupted by several bangs at the door, and then I heard someone yell, "Police!"

I ran downstairs where I was met by two officers at my front door. I could see they had a man in handcuffs face down on the cruiser. They asked me to come out and see whether I could identify him. I was shocked when I saw his face. It was the man I had had dinner with earlier in the evening. Apparently, he had followed me home.

I gasped when the police showed me my front door. He had used a sharp-edged tool to try and pry off my deadbolt.

The wood around it was almost all chipped away. In a few more minutes, he would have been inside.

The incident made me realize I needed to take my celebrity seriously. I had never seen myself as a "star," and honestly, I never liked being called one, but I guess this was the price of fame.

In fact, my public persona seemed mostly to be a magnet for inmates and people with mental issues. My mailbox at the TV station was flooded with letters from men expressing a deep, affectionate love for me or inmates who offered up their release date and suggest I come visit before then if I'd like. Most of my admirers were harmless, but at times the danger could not be ignored.

One afternoon, my news director called me while I was out covering a story. "Come straight to the station," he said authoritatively, insisting my photographer and I not make any stops along the way.

"What's wrong? Is it my mom?" I asked in a high-pitched, nervous voice.

"No. I don't want to upset you now. I'll explain when you get here," he said. "Just make sure you guys don't make any stops. Do you hear me, Romona?"

"Okay, we won't," I said. A hundred thoughts ran through my head.

Pulling into the station in Parma, we saw the place was crawling with police. When I entered the building, the police and my news director were waiting for me.

I quickly learned that a man who had recently been released from a Cleveland mental hospital wanted to kill me. Apparently, he had been calling the receptionist at Channel 43 for weeks, but no one told me. She said the calls had been coming in almost ten times a day. They were never threatening, but she refused to put the calls through to my desk just the same.

This time, the caller told the receptionist he had grown frustrated and was tired of being ignored. He said he was on his way to the station to shoot me.

The police took statements from the receptionist and me, although I could offer no information; to my knowledge, I had never spoken to the caller. One officer remained at the station for a few hours to make sure I was safe. They tried locating the suspect with the information provided by the receptionist. In his earlier calls, he had given her a phone number for me to reach him at.

Police were able to locate him quickly and question him. He lived with his mother, and the story she told police was terrifying and sad. She claimed her son, who was mentally ill, watched me nightly on the ten o'clock news, but he had stopped taking his medication. He had grown increasingly angry and more despondent because he had an earring he insisted I left in his bed. He grew extremely frustrated because I wouldn't come back to get it and because I was ignoring his calls. His mother had told him for weeks that he didn't know me and that the earring he found didn't belong to me. She begged him to take his medicine but to no avail. The police said the mother seemed sincere.

As soon as I heard about the caller, I figured he was probably a lonely man who would never harm me, but the police explained the seriousness of the situation. The man who threatened my life had a criminal record for assault on women. His rap sheet revealed he was about six foot four and over two hundred pounds. His mug shot was frightening. He had deeply set eyes that showed little emotion. It was as if you could see into his soul, and it looked empty.

They took him back to the hospital, and police gave me a copy of his mug shot, along with a stern warning. "If you ever see this man on the street or at an event you attend, walk away as quickly as possible and call police. He will get out again someday and might try to reach out to you," the officer said with certainty. "Let this serve as a warning, Romona. There are a lot of sick and dangerous people out there who will latch onto nice ladies like yourself."

I had always been proud of the fact that I embraced people, learning about their diverse backgrounds and the different cultures that existed in Cleveland. But that day, I became fearful. Police told me the man had access to a gun. His mother owned one, and it was in the house.

There would be several other stalkers throughout my career, but it was part of the business. I didn't want to live a life of fear; I just needed to be careful and have faith that God would protect me.

* * * *

While I hadn't anticipated the dangers associated with celebrity, I had thought that my increasing popularity might lead to finding someone special, a man with whom I could settle down, have children, and create a happy ending. Instead, I found that more temptations came my way. Despite the myths about people in television or entertainment being party animals who frequent lavish events, I was pretty straight-laced. My hair and clothing had changed dramatically since my rural childhood, but underneath it all, I was still a humble and somewhat naïve, shy soul who took pride in holding true to my morals and values. I was determined to never become my own headline by getting into trouble. But trouble can find you if you're not careful.

A woman I didn't know very well—that should have been my first clue—asked me to go to a house party with her. I had met Rena at a social event I hosted for a local magazine. She said one of the Cleveland Browns was throwing the party. Being cautious, as I always was, I asked, "Who's gonna be there?"

"It's supposed to be Cleveland's who's who—politicians, entertainers, other pro ball players," she said.

It sounded like fun, and as a young, single woman, I thought there would be single guys there as well. I figured I could mingle, do some networking, and maybe get some exclusive interviews.

We arrived at the party, which was in a suburb outside of Cleveland. It was an incredible, high-end home with a meticulously manicured lawn. I was impressed when we drove up. I didn't know the athlete personally, but our sports director, Gib Shanley, had interviewed him several times for the ten o'clock news.

Even before we rang the doorbell, we heard the loud music vibrating off the front door. We were greeted by an attractive young lady wearing a dress that I whispered to my girlfriend was way too tight. When we walked inside, the place was rocking. There were people everywhere—in the living room, kitchen, and what looked like a den. It was a nice-looking crowd. The music was cranked up, and the liquor was flowing. I didn't see the athlete who owned the home, but I did see a few familiar faces. Some had appeared on our newscast before. Most of the partygoers were complete strangers, though. Some people danced, while others, mostly couples, walked back to a private room.

Maybe it was the reporter in me, but I asked Rena, "What do you think is in that room? There is a trail of couples heading back there."

She replied, "Maybe it's a VIP area."

"Why couples?" I asked again, even more curious now. "You don't think they're having sex back there, do you?"

"No, girl!" Rena shouted over the music. "Why do you come up with these crazy ideas?"

I remember feeling odd and too plain-Jane, so I accepted a drink when a hostess offered me one. Tall, dark, and handsome interrupted us not long after. He was a perfect gentleman who asked if I wanted to dance. As we danced, I kept thinking how handsome and fit he looked. He tried yelling over the music, asking what I did for a living, and I was equally loud, trying to respond.

He said he was in real estate, visiting from Detroit, and his friend was one of the partygoers. He seemed intrigued by my career and pressed his body closer during our dance to ask for details. When the music stopped, we headed to a corner to talk more. I must admit, my mind shifted to thoughts of getting to know him better, even if he lived a few hours away in Detroit. My initial perception was that he was articulate, in shape, and seemed to have it together.

During our conversation, I noticed couples still flocked to that room in the back. The curiosity was killing me.

"Do you know what's in the room people are lining up to go into?" I asked. "Is it the VIP area?"

"Oh no, that's the coke line! You want a hit?" he asked as he grabbed my hand. "You can go with me. I was about to head back again when I saw you."

Shocked, I pulled away. "No, I don't do that."

"Come on, it will change your life."

"No. It's dangerous."

"Oh, okay, that's cool," he responded. "Then, you want to dance again?"

I couldn't believe he had just asked me to snort cocaine with the same ease as if he had offered me a can of soda. I excused myself, giving him my nice-to-meet-you-and-goodbye line, and rushed through the crowd looking for Rena. When I spotted her, she was deeply engaged in conversation with a man who I must admit was even more handsome than my guy. I knew she would not like what I was about to say.

"Let's go," I whispered in her ear.

She drew back. "Go? Why?"

Her guy friend looked at me and said, "The party just got started. Where do you have to go?"

I looked at him and smiled. "Rena, I really need to talk to you," I said, becoming visibly tense.

She excused herself, telling her friend she'd be right back. "What is wrong, Romona? Why do you look so uptight?"

"I found out what's behind that door. People are going in there to use cocaine. We have to get out of here."

"Why? We're not using."

"But just being associated with people who are…it makes me really nervous, Rena. What if the police come and people are busted for drugs? No one will ever believe I didn't know what was going on here."

"Girl, you worry too much. Let's just enjoy the party," she pleaded. "We don't have to go near that room. And besides, girl, look who's standing in the kitchen waiting for me to return. He is so fine, and he is digging him some Rena!"

I didn't want to be a party pooper, but I didn't give it a second thought. I couldn't put my career in jeopardy. These were the kinds of stories I had reported on—drug busts where everyone involved was either questioned or hauled off to jail. With the big fish in the room—the pro athlete—it would definitely make headlines.

I would have left without Rena, but she had driven that night, so I needed her to take me home. Raising my voice, I again told her we should leave. I knew my friendship with Rena wouldn't last anyway. She was a daredevil who loved to party. She was the type to take risks in the moment and ask questions later. Her persona just didn't mesh with the small-town girl in me who always wanted to know who, what, where, and why before going to a stranger's home.

I was proud that my mom's morals and values still guided me, even if it meant letting a fine man walk away. I was not about to risk a career I had worked so hard for. It was important I not let anyone change the person I was inside. I didn't feel like I had to go along with the crowd to fit in. I was my own person, and if a situation didn't feel right or went against my upbringing and beliefs, I had the power to simply walk away.

Chapter 35
THE STIGMA MUST END

Sometimes, getting yourself out of a bad situation is easier said than done, especially when you don't recognize you're in one.

One winter weekend in 1990, I took a trip with one of my girlfriends to her hometown of Milwaukee. We had plans to go to an afternoon Milwaukee Bucks game. By this time, I had become a huge Cleveland sports fan. The Browns, Cavaliers, Indians—I followed them all. We had great seats for the Bucks, only five rows back. As we enjoyed the game, my girlfriend nudged me to say the star player on the opposing team was checking me out. I looked at him, he smiled, and I smiled back. Every time he came down the court, he glanced over at me. I wondered how he could concentrate on the game and look at me at the same time, but I was flattered.

Later, he sent someone to tell me he'd like my phone number, and I gladly gave him my girlfriend's mom's number, where we were staying. This man was fine, and it didn't hurt that he was a star on an NBA team. I had seen him on several sports talk shows, magazine covers, and commercials. He was tall and handsome. Equally important was that, as an anchor, I had never reported anything bad about him on the news, so I thought he must be a nice guy.

To my surprise, he called shortly after the game. The team was staying overnight and then heading out on a West Coast road trip the next day. He asked if I could have dinner with him that night. Of course I said yes. My girlfriend hovered over my shoulder, listening to every word. He said he'd send a car to pick me up and drive me to the restaurant where he would be waiting for me. Sending a car was a nice touch. I was impressed; no man had ever done that for me.

I wore a satin, cream-colored blouse and a nicely tailored black pantsuit that fit in all the right places. I left a few buttons undone to give me a sexy-but-tasteful look. After all, I was a Christian, and as a respectable anchorwoman, my image was important.

The car arrived around 6:30 p.m. I arrived for dinner at a restaurant right off the entrance to a hotel. As I walked in, he stood up, smiling, and walked toward me. Our eyes locked on each other, as if to say we were both pleased with what we saw.

I was nervous but tried not to show it, thinking the whole time, *I don't think I have ever seen a man looking so good.* He wore a navy suit that looked like it was tailor-made for him. His crisp, white shirt made his dark skin glow in the dim light. It was hard not to be attracted to his physical presence. Not only did he have chiseled good looks, but he also smelled good when he embraced me to say hello.

"You look beautiful, Romona," he said with a smile.

I smiled, pleased he had noticed. "Thank you," I said.

I was surprised by his restaurant of choice. Because it was right off the lobby-lounge area, there was a flurry of people. It was a bit loud—not the intimate setting I had envisioned. A waitress was planted near the wall of the restaurant's entrance and appeared to be waiting for the athlete and me. She smiled, said hello, and quickly seated us in a semi-private area, though we were not completely shielded from other patrons.

From the moment we sat down and opened our menus, fans who spotted him kept walking up to our table, interrupting our conversation. I noticed how polite he was, telling them he was trying to enjoy dinner, if they didn't mind.

I will never forget the mother who actually pulled up a chair to our table, plopped down, and tried to hook up my date with her daughter.

"The two of you attended college together, and she still talks about you. Do you remember her? She was cute, a cheerleader, and took several courses with you," she said, desperately trying to jog his memory.

"Yes, I do remember her," he said. "Please tell her I say hello. You have a nice evening, Miss. I'm going to enjoy my dinner now."

"Do you know her daughter?" I asked because I knew the buzz words for goodbye.

"Hell naw," he said. "I knew it was the only way I could get rid of her. She had gotten comfortable and would have sat here all night. I know the type."

We both laughed. "So is this what the life of an NBA star is like?" I asked.

"Yeah, but I want to talk about you, lovely Romona. I'm loving that outfit. I could hardly concentrate on the game today for looking at you." He leaned over the table to make sure I could hear him. "Are you from Milwaukee? What brought you to town?"

Before I could answer, there was a third and fourth interruption. "This is going to happen all night. We'll never be able to enjoy our dinner. Would you like to go up to my room and order dinner, and we can talk more privately? I'd love to get to know you better," he said with a warm smile.

"Oh, I didn't know you were staying here," I said.

"Yeah, it's convenient to have dinner downstairs since we leave for the West Coast first thing in the morning. Besides, I really don't know the city. I just wanted to meet you and talk to you."

It was about 7:30 p.m. The night was young, and I genuinely wanted to get to know him.

"Sure, we'll order in," I replied.

* * * *

As he shut the hotel door behind me, I took in the immaculate room. The bed was neatly done with plump, white pillows, and light linens were already turned down. There was a sitting area with a handsome chair or two and curtains finished in some sort of light-patterned fabric.

I immediately went in search of the room service menu as he took off his jacket. But before I could turn to ask what he would like for dinner, he came up behind me, startling me. He wrapped his arms tightly around my waist and moved in to kiss me on the neck. I spun around quickly, pushing him back, and my purse went flying across the room.

"This is a little too fast," I said. "I didn't come up here for that."

He grabbed me and pulled me tighter, enveloping me in his massive arms, pressing so tightly against my body I could feel his rib cage. Again, I asked him to stop. I tried pushing him backward toward the door, but I was no match for his superhero-like strength.

He wasn't listening to me. Instead, he used his tight grip to force me down onto the bed.

"I want you to let go of me and let me up right now!" I demanded.

I felt a sudden rush of blood to my head. It felt like it was about to explode. It was in that very moment I knew I was in trouble. The evening I had been so looking forward to was turning into a night of terror. What happened in a matter of minutes seemed like hours.

He was breathing heavily and starting to sweat, mumbling words I couldn't make out.

"No, no…please, let me up…I thought we were ordering dinner," I said as I fought to free my arms.

"Dinner can wait," he whispered in my ear, using the weight of his two-hundred-pound frame to pin me beneath him. One of his arms was pressed so hard against my upper abdomen that I had a hard time breathing, and the screams I was able to utter were becoming faint.

I managed to get one hand free and tried to fight. I begged him to stop, to let me up, as he started to pull at my blouse and suit. He tugged at his belt, telling me to just relax.

"Go with it," he whispered.

My hand was getting tired from trying to fight him off. Finally, with no energy left, my body went limp for a few seconds. I started to cry, thinking, "I'm going to be raped by one of the most popular athletes in the NBA." This man, with a warm smile in public, was really a monster.

He looked so different now. Despite the chilly temperature in the room, sweat dripped from his face, and his eyes stared blankly at me. His white shirt was soiled with my eyeliner, and my blush was smeared all over him. His skin started to feel hot and clammy. *What did I do wrong?* I asked myself in that moment.

Then I snapped to. There was no time for self-pity. I had to get out of there—fast. He had unbelievable strength, holding me down and trying to get my pants off. I did what I used to hear my mom doing late at night: "Lord, Lord, help me!" I cried out. "Lord, please God make him stop."

He was not deterred by my pleas to God. "Go with it. Don't fight me," he uttered.

Suddenly, words came to my rescue. "If you don't get off me, I will tell all of Cleveland and the world what you did to me!"

"Who's gonna believe you?" he murmured, his body still pressed tightly against mine.

"In our short conversation downstairs, you never asked what I did for a living. I'm a television news anchor, a well-respected, churchgoing Christian with a spotless reputation. They *will* believe me," I said, apparently convincingly.

Like a jackrabbit, he sprung up and freed me, telling me to get out as I tried to pull myself together—zipping up my pants, searching for my purse, blowing my breath on my sweat-stained blouse to try and dry it quickly, and finger-combing my hair.

As I headed for the door, I remembered I had been raised to be a lady. I stopped, and to my own amazement, turned and said, "No! You sent a car to pick me up. You *will* send one to take me home, and you *will* walk me downstairs to the car. You will *not* dismiss me as if I'm some whore."

He was shocked at my demands, although he didn't protest. As he walked toward the desk for the phone, I stood next to the door. He didn't touch me again. My position and title had helped me escape being raped in a Milwaukee hotel room.

He called for the car and walked me to the lobby without uttering a word. No "I'm sorry" or "I got carried away." Nothing.

After the episode, I had so many questions: *Why did I seem to attract weirdos? Why would I go into a stranger's hotel room? Why would I feel I knew him well enough to do so after only a short time?*

I knew the old adage "Don't judge a book by its cover," but I was starting to think there was a deeper problem. My actions seemed innocent enough at the time, but I had lived such a sheltered life with my mom that maybe my naïveté hindered my good judgment. As much as I tried blaming myself, though, I couldn't. I was angry. I was embarrassed. But I wasn't the one who had a problem. The man who tried to violate me had the problem, just as my inappropriate teacher did when I was nine years old.

I kept a watchful eye on his career from that night forward. Just one sexual claim against him and I swore I would be there for his victim to tell my story. As a member of the media, I know firsthand the woman is often blamed and shamed in sexual assault cases when the perpetrator is a famous guy.

According to the National Sexual Violence Resource Center, in eight out of ten rape cases, the victim knows the perpetrator, but most women won't report the assault because of shame, fearing they'll be judged, ridiculed, or blamed. What happens to the one in six women who don't have powerful positions who will be raped in their lifetime? Many of their cries for help will be ignored. The stigma of rape has to end.

Chapter 36

HANGING MY HAT
IN CLEVELAND

I was in the driver's seat when it came to my career. Area newspapers and magazines started to call. They wanted to do articles on me and put me on their covers. One of my biggest features was the cover of *Cleveland Magazine* in 1991. The caption read, "Romona Robinson, TV 43's Perfect 10." The cover was called "Romona-mania." The writer talked about my life as an anchor, and more importantly, my charity work in Northeast Ohio and my weekly "Romona's Kids" segments, praising my work with children.

I started receiving community service awards. I had won several Emmy Awards for my anchoring and reporting. I was offered jobs in New York and Los Angeles. It was all so flattering, but Cleveland and its people had me hooked. I loved my work on the air and in the community. I felt as if I were making a difference with children. I told all of my Romona's Kids and everyone I spoke to at schools that I was always there for them and that they could write to me about any problems they had.

Oh boy, did the letters pile in! Most of them were from inner-city girls—black, white, and Hispanic—who felt their environment prevented them from achieving. I especially remember a thirteen-year-old girl who wrote, "Miss Robinson, when you spoke at my school, you said every child should be able to go to college. I still don't think I can because no one in my family has ever gone."

In my response, I channeled my sister, Beulah. "You don't think you can?" I asked. "Oh yes, you can, and you will if you are determined, and here's how…"

I have since gone to many of my Romona's Kids' high school and college graduations.

* * * *

In 1997, after eight years at Channel 43, I decided it was time to go. I would always be thankful for my time there, but it was my dream to work at one of the Big Three network affiliates; Channel 43 was a UPN station.

I decided to hire an agent to test the waters in the market both locally and nationally. To my surprise, he called back a few weeks later, saying there was interest inside and outside the city. I interviewed at a couple of top-five stations, but my heart still belonged to Cleveland.

I eventually decided to sign with Channel 3, the NBC affiliate across town. In March of that year, I was named the new six o'clock and eleven o'clock weeknight anchor. I would eventually make history yet again, becoming the first woman to solo anchor an evening newscast. I enjoyed a nearly fifteen-year successful run.

Chapter 37
POH BLACK FOLKS SHOULD STAY IN THEIR LANE

It was July 23, 2002. A small crowd had gathered around a person seated in front of the dais at the Sheraton City Centre Hotel ballroom in downtown Cleveland. I was curious if all the fuss was over the person I had waited three decades to meet. As I walked closer to the stage through the crowd of several hundred people, her face came into view.

It was her eyes I locked onto first. There was such sincerity about them. Her caramel-colored skin and wavy black hair were unmistakable. She wore a powder-blue suit with a single strand of pearls. At seventy-four years old, she was as beautiful as ever.

"Mrs. King, it is such a pleasure to meet you," I said, bending down to shake her hand as she sat.

"Nice to meet you," she replied warmly.

"I have waited thirty-five years to meet you and your family."

She smiled. "My, what took you so long?"

"I've wanted to thank you and your late husband and your entire family since I was a little girl for your sacrifices, for all of the pain you endured for so many. Thank you," I said again as my voice started to tremble.

She realized I was overwhelmed by the moment and placed her left hand on top of mine.

"You're so welcome," she responded.

Martin Luther King III was standing near Mrs. King. The program was about to start, so I shook his hand quickly and told him how much I admired his father. You got the sense in talking to the Kings that they had been told "thank you" a lot, but they had a way of making you feel as if you were the first person to ever say it. Maybe it was their Southern charm.

Coretta was the keynote speaker that day at the women's luncheon for the SCLC, or Southern Christian Leadership Conference. As I sat there listening to the first lady of the civil rights movement speak about decades of struggle, vision, and victory, I got lost in my thoughts.

I drifted back to the day on Mom's chair when I asked if we could meet Dr. King and his family. My heart began to palpitate as I remembered her answer: "No, baby. Poh black folk like us on this dirt road can never meet people like that." And yet, there they were, standing right in front of me, smiling, shaking my hand, and talking to me. It was a God-created moment.

Chapter 38

A LETTER FROM MR. CRONKITE

On September 27, 2004, I noticed an envelope with the return address "CBS News in New York" as I went through my mail. My hands shook nervously as I tore open the letter and looked at the sender. It was from none other than former CBS news anchor Walter Cronkite, the man himself!

I immediately ran through the halls of the station, reading the letter to anyone and everyone who would listen. A fellow Clevelander had told Mr. Cronkite that he was my idol and inspiration for becoming a journalist, and he actually wrote me. I was flabbergasted. I couldn't believe that Walter Cronkite, who was nearly ninety years old, would take the time to write *me* to wish me well. This was a man I had watched for—well, you know the story. He was an icon, an "untouchable" as far as my hometown was concerned, not someone you could ever expect to emulate.

I rushed to call my mom. I felt like a child all over again. Mom couldn't believe it either. It became clear to me that some of her truths would not be mine; I was holding a personal letter from the man known as a television god. As I looked at the letter, my dreams and entire career came flooding back—all the hard work, the struggles, the tears, and the determination to get to where I was. I wished for a moment that Miss Salone was still alive. I'd call her, too, and tell her—just like I told Mom—that black people like us can become successful news anchors. We can sit next to white people and deliver a newscast. I would rave to her about my letter, and then I'd tell her—respectfully, of course—his name is pronounced *Cronkite!*

Chapter 39
DIVINE INTERVENTION

The excitement in my life continued. In June 2004, I became a married woman. After years of dating and never quite meeting the man for me, it finally happened in 2002.

Rodney's and my love story was one made of undeniable divine intervention. While I was on a girl's weekend in Washington, D.C., I met him in a place Mom said you should never meet a man: in a bar. She used to stress that good men don't hang out in clubs, and they won't make suitable husbands. "You'll only find trouble in those places," she loved to say.

My girlfriend, Marie, and I had flown to D.C. to take in some retail therapy in Georgetown, visit a few monuments, and stay at the Four Seasons.

Upon our arrival, Marie asked our driver where we could meet some nice, eligible bachelors with jobs. We all laughed, but he suggested a club called Zanzibar. I quickly reminded her this was a shop-til-we-drop-and-tour-national-monuments trip; there would no time for clubs.

"I know, I know," Marie snapped. "At least a girl can try."

We giggled. Marie was quite the party girl. We had blanketed this country and a few foreign ones, going to

Fashion Week in New York, heavyweight professional boxing fights in Las Vegas, and attending incredible parties on yachts and islands. However, on this two-day trip, I just wanted to relax.

After six hours of marathon shopping, a wonderful dinner, and a drink at the hotel bar, we were fatigued and called it a night. It would be a sleepless night for me, though. I tossed and turned, struggling to drift off. My eyes shot open in the midst of darkness, a blue light staring me smack in the middle of my eyes. The alarm clock read 12:00. Midnight. *Darn. I've only been asleep for an hour.*

I whispered to Marie, who was sleeping a few feet away. "Marie, are you asleep?"

"No, girl, I've been awake the whole time. You were snoring. You must have really been exhausted," she said, laughing.

"I was, but now you won't believe what I'm thinking."

"What?"

"Let's go to the club the driver told us about where we can meet professional men!"

"Are you serious, Miss 'I Don't Want to Party in D.C.'?"

"Yes, let's go," I said. "It's only midnight. He said they didn't close till about three a.m."

"Girl, you know I'm game."

We sprang out of bed and into our outfits like firemen grabbing their gear in response to a rescue call.

Marie and I were perched at the dimly lit bar by 1:30 a.m., looking single and ready to mingle. Marie called me out on my attire. I wore a form-fitting, black dress that hugged all the right places and came to a few inches above my knee paired with knee-high, black boots.

"Who packs that kind of outfit to tour Washington monuments?" she asked, her brow raised and lip curled.

"Girl, I just knew you would nag me about partying, so I threw an outfit in just in case."

"I still can't believe Miss Prim and Proper woke up at midnight and wanted to go out. Where is my friend, Romona? What have you done with her?" We both laughed.

We got a big kick out of all the pick-up lines we got that night.

"Are you a model?"

"Have we met?"

"You look like someone I know."

"You're so pretty, I'd like to kidnap you."

"Really?" I said to Marie. "Creepy! Where are all of the professional men our driver told us about?"

At one point, we were waved upstairs to the VIP area, but it was lacking. The attractive men were parked against the wall as if they wanted us to come and talk to them or ask them to dance.

"For once, I would love for a man to just walk up and say, 'Hello. What's your name?'" I said. "No lines, just hello."

Five minutes later, a voice over my right shoulder uttered the words, "Hello. What's your name?" No kidding.

As I twisted my body slightly to look up and acknowledge the voice behind me, I was pleasantly surprised. He was handsome. He had caramel-colored skin, stood about six foot six, and was a little north of two hundred pounds with a smile that immediately warmed my heart.

"I'm Rodney," he said, extending his hand.

"I'm Romona, and this is my girlfriend, Marie."

Marie, seated to my left, slyly tapped me on the knee. It was our code that a suitor was not wearing a wedding band. I'm usually an hour into a conversation before I think to look for a ring.

As we talked, my mom's philosophy about men in bars floated in and out of my mind. But, there I was, equipped with my moral compass, speaking with someone who seemed kind and different than the others.

"You mentioned you had two kids. What brings you out tonight?" I asked. "Do you frequent clubs?"

"Not at all, but after months of carpooling, sleepovers, and football practices, I needed some adult time. What brings you here?" he asked.

"I'm visiting from Cleveland. I don't do clubs anymore either, but something woke me up tonight and led me to check out this place."

"Well, I'm glad you did," Rodney responded, now definitely checking out more than my face. But it was a tasteful once-over. He went on. "I was just about to leave shortly after one when the elevator opened, and you stepped out. Your head was down, so I played it off. I rode down and came back up."

The lights started to flicker in the bar, signaling it was nearing three a.m. Rodney and I had unknowingly been talking for more than an hour. I loved the ease and effortless conversation.

"I've never met a woman who knows as much about sports as you do," he said, impressed. "My goodness, you know the starting lineup of most of the NBA and NFL teams. What woman follows sports like that unless they're in the business? You look and sound so polished. What do you do for a living?"

Uh-oh. The dreaded question. My answer usually flipped the conversation to the exciting world of television, which could consume a dinner conversation, creating confusion as to whether my date was interested in me or my occupation.

"You've got to be a sports agent," Rodney pressed.

"What do *you* do?" I shot back.

"I'm an IT guy. A consultant. You've got to have a career in sports," Rodney guessed, still clamoring for an answer. "You know pick and rolls, defensive schemes, screens and traps."

Feeling pressured, I said the first thing that came to mind. "I work for the Cleveland Browns. I'm a manager," I blurted out with sincerity.

"I knew it!" He smiled, pleased that I had verified his suspicions.

Okay, I just lied about what I did for a living to a man I really like.

They say you know right away the man you'll marry when you meet him. I can't describe how I knew at that moment, but as Rodney walked away after we exchanged numbers, a voice said, "Romona, that man will become your husband."

The thought terrified me. I didn't even share it with Marie. I enjoyed his conversation, but I knew little about him, only that he was divorced and was raising two children.

It became a whirlwind, long-distance courtship, complicated by the fact that I was still lying about what I did for a living. I would fly to D.C. and stay in a hotel, not wanting to set a bad example by staying with Rodney and his children. I refused to let him visit me in Cleveland, always finding an excuse to protect my cover. We talked on the phone morning, noon, and night. Rodney would ask why I worked so late with the Browns, so during his nine p.m. calls, I found a quiet corner in the newsroom where I could cuddle up with my cell phone.

The jig was up the day his teenage son asked if I could get quarterback Tim Couch's autograph. I could no longer lie. It was one thing to keep up the charade with Rodney, but I couldn't lie to his son.

I remember vividly when I broke the news to him. I worried it might taint me in his eyes or flag me as a liar. I explained that I had been burned in past relationships by guys pretending to be into me because of my wealth or because I could elevate their career or serve as expensive arm candy. To my surprise, he wasn't angry. He said he saw my heart and the beauty I possessed inside.

We were married two years later. I had been blessed to discover what it truly meant to love and be loved.

Chapter 40
ROMONA'S CHILDREN

Rodney was the man I had waited to spend my life with and start a family with, but had I waited too long? I was forty-two years old. My mom had her last child at forty-three, so the doctors thought I had a shot at getting pregnant, especially since I had no health problems. We would try the old-fashioned way and then use modern medicine if we needed to.

I conceived three times over six years, only to have each pregnancy fail. My heart was crushed. After dozens of doctor visits, tens of thousands of dollars, marathon-scheduled shots, popping fertility pills, and in vitro fertilization, my body couldn't take it anymore. The stress was too much, and the counseling sessions and pep talks from friends who had children seemed to leave me even more depressed. My husband and I prayed together, along with members of our church, that God might grant us a child, but when it didn't happen, I sank into a deep depression. I questioned myself as a woman. It seemed so natural for my sisters and girlfriends who had several children. Why had it escaped me? I knew when I made the decision to wait for the right man before having children that it would be a risk.

I knew I needed professional help, but I couldn't ask for it. For me, it would have been a sign of weakness. Sharing all of my heartache and pain with a complete stranger just seemed impossible to do. My friends and I had talked about therapists in the past. In those conversations, none of my black friends had ever sought help. It seemed we had grown up being taught or believing we were weak if we visited a so-called shrink. I wasn't sure if that was a cultural belief, but a few of my white colleagues swore by therapy.

Instead, I tried to pray away the pain in order to convince myself that I was strong enough to endure my repeated losses. I would go home, curl up in the usual fetal position, and cry myself to sleep night after night, month after month, careful not to let my husband hear me. I knew he would worry, and even though he was extremely supportive, nothing could cure my longing for a child.

I recall that each miscarriage was marked by gruesome headlines I read at work:

"Police find a newborn in a dumpster."

"Four children are killed by their father."

After losing my third child, I returned to work the next day because it was an important ratings month. No one at Channel 3 knew. I couldn't talk about my loss without becoming a basket case, so I kept it between my husband and me.

Before I went into work at the station, I gave myself a boisterous pep talk, as I did after each loss. "Romona, you are strong." I smiled and looked into the mirror. "You are okay. You can handle this, girl. Sarah bore a child for Abraham in their old age."

But Sarah was barren until she was almost ninety. I screamed into my mirror as the tears began to flow. "I want babies now! How could I lose all of my babies?"

I sunk slowly onto my cold, tiled bathroom floor. The devil had shown up and was showing out again. "You're weak, you're barren, you can't carry a child! What kind of woman can't bear children? Look at you, on the floor like a pathetic child! You better not tell anyone about this. They're gonna say you're weak, you're crazy! They're laughing at you, Romona!"

I wish I could lie and say that I was just distraught, that my emotions had simply gotten the better of me as I let the devil in my ear, but I had danced to this tune before. A gaping wound had opened in my heart in 1999. I'd had a child then. She was the joy of my life, the center of my being, but she was snatched from me like a thief in the night. It was a sudden loss I had no time to prepare for.

One day, my younger sister in Missouri called me. She was hysterical, begging me to take my niece, fearing DFS—the Division of Family Services—would place her daughter in foster care. Unbeknownst to me, my sister, who had struggled with drug abuse since she dropped out of college, relapsed. The forces of darkness once again took her to a place of drugs and despair. Reportedly, she had been leaving her two children home alone. A neighbor called the police to report her and also said that drugs were in the home. Social workers showed up quickly and put pressure on her to improve her situation. She was required to enter treatment, and there would be repeated home visits. Her son went to stay with his dad, and she pleaded with me to take her daughter.

As a single woman with a high-powered, demanding television career, I knew nothing about raising a child, but it was my niece, and I had to do it. My sister promised me it would only be six months until she completed treatment and got her life back on track. So, I flew my niece to Cleveland, and I was instantly the mother of a seven-year-old.

I remember just looking at her beautiful, smooth, dark skin, which reminded me of chocolate mousse. Her hair was pulled tightly into two ponytails adorned with lavender ribbons. As we entered my home, the fear was visible in her curious brown eyes. She reminded me of a newborn doe—standing still, then slowly moving about, taking baby steps in her unfamiliar surroundings. I quickly enveloped her tiny, four-foot-three-inch frame into my arms to reassure her it was going to be okay and that she was safe.

She had arrived with an awful cold, and I had no idea what to do. I had given her some over-the-counter medicine, but she seemed to be getting worse—sweating, coughing, and looking peaked. *Do I take her to the emergency room?*

I decided to call my girlfriend, who had three kids.

"Did you take her temperature?" she asked.

"I didn't think to check," I told her. She laughed, realizing I had a lot to learn.

Six months of nurturing my niece turned into three and a half of the most satisfying years of my life. My niece and I were total opposites. I loved high fashion, and she preferred jeans and tennis shoes. I enjoyed steak and lobster; she always wanted McDonald's. But the love we shared for one another was undeniable. You hardly saw one of us without the other. We created our own special, corny song we'd sing to each other before school each morning: "Together, together is how we'll always be…Together, forever, it's just you and me."

When she was ten and a half years old, I started saving for her college education. We continued our prayer for her mom at night. One morning, my niece asked me something that came as a total shock.

"Aunt, can I call you Mommy?"

Silence. I didn't have an immediate answer.

"You're like my mommy," she went on. "You've been raising me for three years, you love me, you feed me, you buy me clothes and send me to school and take me to church." She smiled, waiting for my response.

After a deep breath, I mustered up the nerve to speak. "Well, I love you like you're my little girl, but I'm…you know…I'm your aunt. My sister is your mom," I awkwardly explained, even though in my heart, I had already adopted her as my own.

"I still love Mommy, too, but can't I have two mommies?"

I was thinking that at ten years old, this child was mature beyond her years.

"I love that idea! Yes, I'm Mommy number two!" I smiled and gave her a long embrace.

My sister called to check in from time to time to see how my niece was doing, but she never had a time frame of when or if she might be ready to care for her again. So many times I gave her money to get by. She always needed money for bills. Some were legitimate, and others I knew were a lie. I bought her a car to go back to college to pursue her degree. She trashed the car and used my money to buy drugs, according to her counselor and the caseworker assigned to help her in rehab.

They told me, "Romona, you can't help your sister by giving her money. You are a huge part of the problem. You've become an enabler. She knows you're her fallback. You must stop giving to her now."

Those words stung. I always thought I was saving my sister from homelessness, from going hungry, from not having a roof over her head, and now to think I've been part of the problem.

One of my most memorable phone calls with my sister was a prayer session. I cried as I reminded her that we were both baptized of water, that we were children of God, and I tried to pray away the demon she said had taken ahold of her.

"You don't understand addiction, Romona. He is my friend. He makes me feel good," she explained.

"But you're so intelligent. Just tell me why," I sobbed. I begged her to stop using and explain how her love of this drug was more important than her God and her children.

I just assumed I'd be putting my niece through high school and sending her off to college. My attorney had been pressuring me to make it legal and formally adopt my niece. However, I shunned his advice, always remembering that I had promised my sister that when she got healthy and found a stable job and place to live, I would return her child. In fact, my sister had made me promise I would give her baby back when she was better, stressing she chose me because she knew she could trust me.

In the summer of 2002, I sent my niece home for a week to spend time with her grandmother and cousins. When I got the call, it hit me like a ton of bricks.

"She's gone," Peach said.

"Gone where? She's missing?" I asked, panic-stricken. My heart wanted out of my chest.

"No. Her mom drove up and told her to get in the car, and she left," said Peach, seemingly in shock. "The conversation was short. She said she had a job, she had her son back, and she wanted her daughter. Then she drove off."

Before I could fully process what I was hearing, I hung up and phoned my attorney.

"Romona, this is what I wanted to protect you from," he said sympathetically. "You have no legal rights to your niece. There is a course of action we can take if we can prove she's still not fit to care for her daughter or if she's still using drugs. We can call Missouri authorities and have them hunt her down, but be prepared for a long fight. Your sister has all the rights, and if she now has a home and can provide for your niece, she didn't need your permission to take her."

It would be a couple of years before I learned of my sister's whereabouts, and it would take many more to mend our relationship.

I still recall the heart-pounding moment when I saw my niece for the first time after she was taken from me. It was in Mom's kitchen. My sister and I were coincidentally visiting her at the same time. My niece was a healthy, happy, no longer shy teenager who hadn't lost her infectious smile. Even at fifteen, she wanted to know if I still remembered our favorite song. A wave of emotion coursed through me as she grabbed my hands. We sang it to each other, just as we had done so many times before. The sudden memory of motherhood came rushing back, and I mourned the years I had missed out on and lost...

* * * *

So there I lay, re-experiencing her loss, collapsed on my bathroom floor in Cleveland. My body was drenched in my own tears and sweat after what seemed like an eternity of uncontrollable chaos in my head. Then a voice said, "Romona, rise. Get up off the floor."

"God, if it's you, help me," I said as I began to pull myself together. "I don't want to be eighty or ninety like Sarah. I want a baby now! Why have you taken my babies? Why have you allowed such heartache and pain over and over again? What did I do to deserve this? Don't you love me?"

I continued to stare in the mirror as if God were right there in front of me. "I've tried to live the right kind of life. I accepted you as my Lord and Savior. I've helped those less fortunate. I work with children, I volunteer for many charities, I attend church. I've done everything to please you."

I went on for several minutes with "I…I…I." By then, the work hour was nearing, and the pity party needed to end. There would be no answer from God.

"Romona, today you won't cry. You won't cry," I told myself. "You will smile, you will laugh, and you will tell everyone you're great, you couldn't be better."

I even rehearsed answers I might give to certain questions if someone detected my sadness. My colleagues knew I loved to laugh and talk sports, and if I were uncharacteristically quiet, it would not go unnoticed.

"There's a baby boom at a Cleveland hospital. Multiple sets of twins were born on the same day," the tease read. As I recited the words at the anchor desk, my heart sank. I felt hollow inside. A dark emptiness consumed my body, but somehow I managed to read the story with a look of joy on my face and even added my congratulations to the families, which wasn't written on the teleprompter.

However, what would ultimately and unknowingly push me to the edge were the words of strangers.

One woman stopped me at a local mall. "I saw your wedding on television. I've been watching and waiting for you to get pregnant. When are the children coming?" she prodded, smiling as if she were about to get a scoop. "I love your work with Romona's Kids," she went on. "You're going to be such a great mom. I was watching a few months back, and your breasts seemed rather large and your tiny waist seemed fuller. I told my husband, 'She's pregnant, I know it!' But looking at you now, you're so skinny it's obvious you're not. I have two of my own, and there's nothing like being a mom."

"It's nice to know. Thank you," I replied. "It was very nice to meet you." She, of course, had no way of knowing the turmoil I was in and that yes, a few months back, I had been pregnant.

* * * *

My heartache never fully went away, but years later, an unexpected message brought me an incredible peace.

One of my Romona's Kids messaged me on Facebook: "Miss Robinson, I hope you never leave Cleveland. We need you."

And there it was. *Had God not granted me children because He knew if I had my own I wouldn't have time for the four thousand kids I've met and spent time with over the last twenty-nine years?*

I'd had the opportunity to nurture and provide hope and encouragement to so many youngsters each week. They shared their hopes and dreams with me. I strived to provide for them wisdom and insight. We laughed and danced and just talked. It was such a blessing that the parents of Northeast Ohio had shared their children with me and entrusted them to me. They filled my heart with joy.

I suddenly started to feel full again. The nagging ache of wanting a child had dissipated. I couldn't bear children, but I had given birth to God's calling for me. I finally understood the enormity of the help and hope I could provide for children who needed it.

Chapter 41
PRESIDENTIAL EXCLUSIVE

In April 2011, I was taking the two-mile cab ride from my hotel to 1600 Pennsylvania Avenue in Washington, D.C. I was answering a text from my sister.

"Are you nervous?" she asked.

"Surprisingly no, I'm not," I replied.

I was about to interview President of the United States Barack Obama. It was an uncommon, sit-down interview at the White House. Presidents rarely grant one-on-one interviews to local reporters. I'm still not quite sure how it happened.

A station manager and I were talking about my bucket list. I told him there were only a few things in the business I still wanted to do. Number one on my list was to have a one-on-one interview with the president of the United States. Unbeknownst to me, he pulled some strings, and a few months later, the White House called.

My producer and I cleared security and were led through a back entrance into the White House Briefing Room to wait for the interview.

"This is the room we've probably seen most often on television," said my producer.

It seemed so much smaller than on TV. This room housed the podium that the president or White House press secretary used to speak to the media. Three middle-aged white male reporters from other network news outlets were there waiting for the news briefing, but I was the only one waiting to interview the president. I thought back to Walter Cronkite for a moment, and I wondered whether this was the same room where he had sat, waiting for briefings or interviews with former presidents.

Suddenly, I felt like a little girl again with nothing but a hope and a prayer of becoming a journalist. I was about to interview the most powerful man in the world.

After ten minutes, we were escorted to the Diplomatic Room. The Diplomatic Room is one of three oval rooms that serves as the primary entrance for the first family, and it is a reception room where foreign ambassadors are greeted. It was decked out in priceless antiques and Federal-era furnishings (my producer and I were told not to sit on the fragile, yellow, damask chairs). I was immediately drawn to panoramic views of the walls decorated with antique French wallpaper. The blue-and-gold carpet incorporated the seals, or coats of arms, of the fifty United States.

I noticed a dish for the presidential first dog, Bo. I was hoping he might trot in, not only because I love dogs, but also because I thought he might calm my nerves.

Soon, a White House staffer walked in and called my name. "Romona Robinson from Cleveland, the president will see you now." I took a deep breath as I rose from my chair, tugging on my royal-blue jacket and black top, adjusting my black pencil skirt as I followed closely behind her.

We came to the entrance of the White House Map Room. The Dalai Lama had been there about a year earlier. It was the room used by President Franklin D. Roosevelt as a situation room to keep track of the events of World War II. President Richard Nixon had it converted into a sitting room. But it now served as a private meeting room for the president or first lady.

I walked in, and there he was: President Barack Obama. He was smiling at me, surrounded by the Secret Service and a cadre of staffers. Even for a journalist, the moment was surreal. I suddenly had a bad case of nerves, but thankfully, as soon as we were introduced, the president asked, "So, Romona, where are your people from?"

The question surprised me. I'd been vetted weeks before, so surely he knew all about me.

"My mom and nine sisters and one brother are scattered throughout Missouri, Michigan, and Texas," I replied.

"Oh my! Ten girls and one boy, the poor fella," he laughed.

My mom and sisters all wanted me to report back if the president was as fine as he looked on television, but as a journalist, my objectivity and unbiased reporting would not be swayed by my family's love for the president.

I knew before the interview I would only get about fifteen minutes, so I dove right in, asking him about issues plaguing Northeast Ohio. We talked about skyrocketing gas prices, surging unemployment, and Cleveland's county corruption.

After the interview, one thing was evident: It was impossible not to like the president. He stood up and flashed that boyish grin when I told him I was a huge Cleveland Cavaliers fan, even though I knew he loved the Chicago Bulls. We kibitzed briefly about the upcoming NBA playoffs and then said goodbye.

After the interview, all I could say was, "Wow." From my mom's chair in Wilson City to a seat next to the president at the White House...who could have known? But I knew the answer—God did.

Chapter 42

AN UNEXPECTED PATH

Several months later, in December 2011, when my contract at Channel 3 ended, I was out of a job once again. My unemployment didn't last long, though. I joined Channel 19, the local CBS affiliate in Cleveland, just three weeks later.

My decision to work for WOIO-TV 19 was a huge source of concern for many viewers and was widely talked and written about.

"Romona, what are you doing?" a Channel 3 viewer wrote. "Are you really going to sell out and work for that trashy station?"

Another caller suggested I was selling my soul to the devil.

Channel 19—19 Action News, as it was branded—was considered tabloid or "shock TV" news. It had been the butt of jokes and ridicule for years after adopting the format of fast-paced, in-your-face reporting, chasing down people for interviews. Reporters were encouraged to use name-calling in their stories. Many felt my conservative style would not mesh with such an overt storytelling style, and they were right.

It was shortly before Christmas when I met with Channel 19 news director, Dan Salamone. I mostly did it to be kind because I told my attorney / agent I would, but I had no intention of working for a station that did not represent the integrity and trust I had worked so hard to build in Cleveland. I even said to Rodney as I left for my lunchtime meeting with Dan, "This shouldn't take long. I could never work for them."

When I walked into the restaurant for our meeting, Dan stood to greet me. "Hello, Romona," he said with a smile.

"It's a pleasure to meet you," I responded.

After a little small talk, what he said next floored me. "Romona, let me cut to the chase. We've experimented with the action news format for ten years, and while we've seen a little success here and there, it's just not working. Viewers are telling us they want a change, and this is where you come in."

He had suddenly piqued my curiosity. I leaned in to listen to more.

"We want to go more mainstream. We want Channel 19 to represent integrity, respect, trust, and compassion for the city, all of the things we know you represent. We feel you can instantly bring those qualities to our revamped newscasts."

I was astonished. This was not the meeting I was expecting. I was speechless for a moment. All I could manage was, "Wow, wow."

Dan went on to explain his plans to change the news brand and the hard work it would require. I thanked him for lunch and said he would be hearing from my attorney.

As I walked to my car to return home, I couldn't believe what had come over me. I was no longer thinking about the other local interview I had just had or the upcoming job interview I had out of town.

In the restaurant parking lot, I called Rodney.

"How did it go?" he asked.

"You won't believe this…" I started.

"What? What's wrong?"

"That's the problem. Nothing is wrong."

"Are you okay, honey?" he asked.

"I think I might want to work for Channel 19." Hearing myself say it shocked me.

"Really? Get home so we can talk."

Weeks later, and after much prayer and talking with my pastor, family, friends, and Dan, I agreed to become the primary anchor for Channel 19. I had the opportunity to try and help change the culture of a television station by representing God's goodness and grace that lives within me by going down His charted path.

Five years later, the now Cleveland 19 News is not the butt of jokes; it's a place my colleagues and I can hold our heads high as we work to deliver professional, credible, and informative newscasts each day.

Chapter 43
FAITH OVER FEAR

It was April 2013, a week after Mom's stroke. I was pressed tightly next to her. This time, we were not on her big, comfy, living room chair where we met every evening to watch Walter Cronkite. Instead, we were in her shower in a hospital in Columbia, Missouri, my body awkwardly twisted like a contortionist between her hospital chair and the shower walls.

Due to paralysis from the stroke, she could no longer bathe herself. She wasn't comfortable with strangers touching her in the most intimate ways of a bath, so she asked me to shower her.

The water rolled down her still-beautiful, dark skin, her back revealing the strength and muscle tone of a much younger woman. As I gently rolled the soap-soaked sponge over her seventy-nine-year-old body, all I could see were invisible stories. With each stroke, I was reminded of all she had endured, all she had given up so her children might escape poverty.

It was our quiet time, just like when I was a little girl, but now our roles were reversed. I was bathing her, providing words of faith and hope that she could overcome the paralysis she had suffered, that she would walk again one day under her own strength.

Her faith was failing her. She rambled about not being sure whether God would give her back her mobility and independence. She seemed to be searching for her favorite sayings to describe her feelings as she incoherently talked about God, but on that day, none of her words expressed faith. "God, might bring me back from this…Maybe God's done givin' up on me…I just don't know if I'm gonna walk again…"

Her fear was contagious. In that moment, I too began to doubt God's favor. The woman who had always been a pillar of strength seemed vulnerable to self-doubt. Suddenly, she snapped at me for rubbing too gently and asked me to scrub harder. Tears rolled down my face. Seeing my mom in such a weakened state was uncharted territory. I was careful not to let her see I had become emotional. I had to encourage her now.

Like a fired-up preacher on Sunday morning who was feeling the Holy Ghost, I wiped away my tears and started thanking and praising her.

"Mom, thank you for all of the lessons. Thank you for breaking the chains of poverty that held our family back from economic success for decades. Thank you for dreaming of a world outside our limited existence. You could have thrown your hands up with eleven children and said, 'I can't do this,' but you didn't. I thank you for being a nurturing, strict parent, for pushing and protecting me. I especially thank you for introducing me to my idol, Walter Cronkite. But, most importantly, I thank you for planting the seed of faith that has grown within me so that I might spread it to others. Thank you for showing me that when faced with the fork in the road, to always pray and ask God to guide me. I praise you for giving me the greatest gift of all—for teaching me to love the Lord and to take the path of faith, not fear."

Epilogue

As I reread Mr. Cronkite's letter, it reveals something I had never imagined. All these years, I thought I wanted to be just like Mr. Cronkite, but I now believe that what I really wanted was a voice, a platform on which to speak. I wanted an audience and the ability to tell useful and meaningful stories that could change lives. In telling my own story, I hope to inspire and encourage others. Like Mr. Cronkite, I am interested in great storytelling and solid journalism. I am interested in touching the lives of people.

Eddie Levert, the singer for the legendary O'Jays, told me something during an interview that encapsulates what my journey has been about. He said, "God comes first, then yourself, and then the people He put you on this Earth to serve."

For days I thought about what Mr. Levert said. This book, I believe, isn't about me at all. It's about *you*, the person who is reading it. I hope it fills you with spiritual nourishment and faith in mankind. I pray it inspires you to follow your dreams and to take risks to achieve them. I pray that young men and women and single and divorced moms know it's possible to raise healthy, happy, and successful children if you're willing to do the hard work.

I know now that I have been on a carefully planned path, on a mission. My journey has prepared me for this, to tell my own story in the hope of encouraging and inspiring others. For decades, like most people, I've had to face adversity. I've had to work harder and smarter to succeed. I thought I was in charge of my destiny.

However, in chronicling my story, I have had the revelation that my life hasn't just been about me. God has been at work the whole time, grooming me since I was six years old to testify and praise Him for His work in my life, helping me get through the hurt and the pain.

I think back to the prisoners I encountered at Missouri State Penitentiary all those years ago and the words they shouted at me. Was I supposed to see them up close? Were they supposed to see me up close? Should I have said more to them? Was our brief encounter a message from the Lord about how different roads can lead to good or evil?

And what about the Ku Klux Klan rally? Had the Lord placed me there to toughen me up and strengthen my faith?

When I struggled to free myself from a man who wanted to violate me, did God enter the room because I called out for Him to help, giving me the words I needed to free myself?

The rewards and triumphs in my own life have been plenty, and I pray yours are, too. But there has also been a lot of hurt, struggle, and disappointment. Just remember: Without risk, there is no opportunity for reward.

Then Peter called to him, "Lord, if it's really you, tell me to come to you, walking on the water."

"Yes, come," Jesus said.

So Peter went over the side of the boat and walked on the water toward Jesus. But when he saw the strong wind and the waves, he was terrified and began to sink. "Save me, Lord!" he shouted.

Jesus immediately reached out and grabbed him. "You have so little faith," Jesus said. "Why did you doubt me?" When they climbed back into the boat, the wind stopped.

—Matthew 14:28-32 (NLT)

Acknowledgments

Writing my first book has been a ten-year labor of love, a project that I am sure tested the patience of my family and friends. They'd never admit it, but they're probably thrilled I'm no longer nagging them about dates, times, and places.

It's impossible to list everyone who pushed me with pep talks and prayer, but I thank all of you.

My dear friend, Avery Friedman, you believed in my story from the beginning, and I'm grateful for your immeasurable encouragement.

New York Times best-selling author, Regina Brett, you have been a godsend. Not only did you freely share valuable information about publishing, you named my book after reading a few chapters—something that had eluded me for a decade after I first began to write it! In the midst of your own hectic schedule, you paused to read my manuscript and offered a glowing testimony.

Stuart Warner, my writing coach, you helped me give life to my journey by reminding me to take the reader to the scene and let them hear, feel, smell, and see the action.

Deb Ring, my first talented copy editor, you tackled my raw, unfinished manuscript and encouraged me to just keep writing.

Thank you to my spiritual leaders, Bishop & Pastor Larry Macon Sr., Rev. Otis Moss Jr., and Dr. Rev. Marvin McMickle. Your support, opinions, and advice were critical.

Best-selling author, George Fraser, you immediately offered up a to-do list and pitfalls to avoid when publishing. Your direct honesty was appreciated.

Nancy Lerner Fisher, your encouragement from the start to go for it was that tiny voice I'd hear when I became discouraged.

Emilia Pollina, Kelly Banks, Marie Johnson, Kim Johnson, and Melanie Kennedy. Wow. My dear friends, I asked for your honest feedback on the book and boy, did you deliver. The producer in some of you flourished with ideas, and I loved every minute of it! You exemplify the meaning of true friendship.

To my news director at WOIO, Fred D'Ambrosi, you weren't my target audience, but your enjoyment of the stories proved the book has a broader appeal.

Jodie Greenberg, my incredible editor, you helped transform my manuscript with your talent and honesty and provided the clarity I needed. It was a joy to work with you.

Lisa Umina and the entire Halo Publishing International team, thank you for your guidance on this journey. Your professionalism and attention to detail created an enjoyable publishing experience.

My sister-in-law, Ramona Tyler, your feedback and constructive criticism were huge.

To my sister, Melissa, I know there were days you didn't want to answer the phone, fearing another steady diet of the book, yet you were always there to listen.

I am grateful for all of my siblings, who have always had my back. From protecting me on the playground from bullies to being my biggest cheerleaders, your love and support mean more than you know.

My loving husband, Rodney. I asked God for a man who would love and respect me and wow, did He provide. He even threw in some extras—a man who is an incredible cook and enjoys karaoke more than me! Thanks for taking this journey with me.

Most of all, I dedicate this book to Mom. I am who I am because of you and your strict teachings. You introduced me to my Lord and Savior Jesus Christ and my idol, Walter Cronkite. The Bible says in Proverbs 22:6, "Train up a child in the way he should go, and when he is old he will not depart from it." I am a living testament of the Scripture. I'm not perfect, but no matter the success I've achieved, I continue to put God first in my life. I love you for your protection, discipline, and most of all, being there.

ABOUT ROMONA

Romona Robinson is an eight-time Emmy Award-winning journalist, with thirty years of public speaking experience. She was the first black female to anchor an evening broadcast in Cleveland. She was also the first woman to solo anchor an evening newscast in the city. She is one of the most well-respected and admired journalists in Northeast Ohio, having earned the trust of viewers for her integrity and unbiased reporting. As a journalist, Romona has traveled the country, covering presidents and world leaders, including Nelson Mandela and the late Ronald Reagan. In 2011, she garnered a rare, exclusive interview with President Barack Obama.

Along with her colleagues at station WOIO-TV 19 where she serves as primary anchor, Romona won the coveted

Edward R. Murrow Award in 2014. She was inducted into the Press Club of Cleveland's Journalism Hall of Fame in 2016 and had the honor of receiving EWAW's Alpha Woman Award in 2017, which is given to women who exemplify strength in their field and use it to empower other women.

One of Romona's most gratifying achievements was creating Romona's Kids, a program-turned-institution in Cleveland that not only brings attention to children in the community but also helps them realize their dreams and potential. For twenty years, Romona has also served as the honorary chair of the Komen Race for the Cure, helping to bring awareness and hope to countless women. Romona's tireless work with children and her dedication to diversity issues have earned her such prestigious awards as the YWCA's Women of Achievement Award and The Diversity in Media Award.

Romona is also recognized for her powerful, dynamic messages as a motivational speaker. Raised by a single mom with little hope of realizing her dream of becoming a journalist, Romona went on to earn a Bachelor of Science degree in broadcast journalism from Lincoln University in Jefferson City, Missouri. Now, Romona is frequently called upon to speak to children and women who need positive messages of faith, hope, determination, and perseverance. She has blanketed the state of Ohio and other parts of the nation, attending events from corporate affairs to meetings of various women's organizations. She firmly believes that success is not measured by your paycheck but by how you pay back God's gift.